GOD ON T

C000091969

Dedicated to all those individual pioneers
who have paved the way.
With thanks to Lindsey MacFarlane, Jo Wells, Helen Rodgers
and my trusty parents
for all their help in pulling this book together.
Much appreciated.

God on the Road

ANDY FROST

survivor

ISBN 978–1–84291–342–0

Design for cover by
www.wildfirestudios.co.uk

Survivor is an imprint of
KINGSWAY COMMUNICATIONS LTD
Lottbridge Drove, Eastbourne BN23 6NT, England.
Email: info@survivor.co.uk

Printed in the USA

Contents

Foreword

The travel writer Tim Cahill says that 'a journey is best measured in friends rather than miles'. *God on the Road* is certainly such a story. Andy Frost's expedition around south west Europe was more than just a road trip, and became more than a standard missions trip too. Andy describes many amazing places so vividly you can almost taste the salt in the air, but along the way he also introduces some amazing people. And it is the interaction between these people that sets the pace as he describes the friendships they forge on the road, and the deepening of his own friendship with God on the inner journey that is the ultimate adventure for us all.

As a long-haired student I undertook a similar trip around Europe a number of years ago, although I confess that my motives were a lot less altruistic than Andy's. However, my beach-bumming, back-packing, hitch-hiking fun was hijacked one night without warning by (of all things) a supernatural vision! That night on the cliff-tops of Cape St Vincent, I heard a buzzing sound and felt electric pulses charge through my body. I was alarmed (treacherous cliff tops are generally pretty lousy places to start shaking). But then, with my eyes wide open, I found that I could see not just our tent, not just the inauspicious swathes of scrubland rolling away from my feet, but also, somehow super-imposed upon all this, the pages of a schoolboy atlas. And from the pages of the atlas, I could see an army of young people aris-ing. Thousands upon thousands, standing in silence, loyal and somber, anticipating their orders.

That simple, scary vision changed my life. For starters it trig-gered the events which gave rise to the 24-7 prayer movement which – last time we counted - was in 63 nations. Andy's journey around Europe with his friends is also, I believe, another small part of the fulfilment of this great mobilisation in our generation. However, the army cannot and must not be claimed by any single initiative, personality or brand. It is commissioned and coordinated solely by God. He alone is our Commander-in-Chief.

Mobility and a thirst for adventure are marks of the new mili-tia but its soldiers are also relational and connected – comrades at arms. Most of all, they march on their knees, stand up for the poor and walk barefoot with those who don't yet know Jesus. These traits are the heartbeat of Andy's band of vagrants as they traverse one corner of this Late, Great, Dark Continent. Theirs is a story measured in friendship and you'll find that it's told in a refreshingly conversational style. We cannot afford to patronise such tales. Without stories and the discipline of storytelling there would be no bible! The winding narratives of our friendships, our journeys, our many mistakes and occasional moments of serendipity – these are the very vessels which convey in every generation the reality of divinity clothed in this glorious befuddle-ment of bumbling humanity.

Andy's story is a journey of miles and friends but also of reve-lation. The road trip becomes a mission trip and the tourists become pilgrims. In fact, by some divine process of osmosis, they themselves gradually become the mission field! I have a hunch that this idea of pilgrimage may well be one of the great forgotten keys which could help unlock the meaning of mission in our contemporary context. Tourists travel to experience and to collect. True pilgrims travel to find something of God and when they find Him they give themselves away in worship. Too often our attempts at mission have reversed this honest quest. We have tended to travel in order to condemn other cultures and people, failing to see that God is often already in them, and that our job is not to impose something from outside but to recognise and baptise something already within. 'The kingdom of God,' said Jesus to a cynical bunch of Pharisees, 'is within you' (Luke 17:21).

More and more people in our generation are embarking upon pilgrimage. Yesterday I received an email from a couple who quit their jobs earlier this year and packed their two kids into an old van to start travelling prayerfully around Europe like ancient friars, seeking God and making friends. Right now they're in Macedonia where they will spend the winter helping to start a new church in Skopje for young adults. Last week I met a graphic designer with long, dark dreadlocks who had quit his job and was about to jump on a plane to New Zealand where he believes God is calling him to live for awhile, though he doesn't yet know why.

Jesus said that those born of the Spirit would be unpredictable and untamable: 'The wind blows wherever it pleases. You hear its sound, but you cannot tell where it comes from or where it is going. So it is with everyone born of the Spirit' (John 3:8). As the title of this book reveals, God in heaven is also, by his Spirit, on the road. Mobility, mission, worship, friendship – these are all marks of the army that God is commissioning and if it can involve a surf board, so much the better. Andy's book – no, Andy friendships – are very much part of that stirring, and I therefore commend him and his story to you and your friends on the journey of your lives.

Lord, thank you that you really are mobilising us to pray, to befriend, to pioneer and to make a stand, especially for Europe at this time. I pray that you would stir our hearts to undertake new journeys – literal or spiritual – measured in friendships and not in miles. Please undermine our complacency, shake us and wake us, so that our lives may count in the wild adventure of your Kingdom. Amen.

I'll see you on the road!

Pete Greig

The Road Trip Long-Board Team

Formal introductions are always good, so here are the twelve other intrepid missioners who embarked on the entire three-week adventure around France, Spain and Portugal with me. . .

The lads . . .

Steve Cotton: the kind of guy who loves deep and meaningfuls. He can talk for hours about the gritty issues of life and faith. Combined with a boyish sense of adventure that wants to explore everything and have a laugh, he is the complex, intriguing and loveable Ste.

Jon Hans: one man and his guitar. Jon grew up in Indonesia and loves surfing, eating fast food and telling stories of epic wipe-outs. Presently residing in Hollywood, he is one of those friends who could one day be a famous rock 'n' roll star. The ladies dig him.

Chris Stone: with a video camera forever perched in his hand, Chris is a contemplative guy who boasts a subtle wisdom about life. Always offering a thought-provoker, his prayerful nature and artistic flair shine through.

Dave Blackgrove: aka 'DJ Dave', with his proper south London accent and his wheeling-and-dealing-type talk, he should have starred in *Only Fools and Horses*. Always smiling, and very useful for rescuing cars during sandstorms.

The ladies . . .

Lisa Clements: a total Jesus freak whom you just love to be around. No matter where God leads her, Essex is firmly in her heart (and her accent too!). Confident to talk to anyone – only Lisa would be able to start a water fight between OAPs in Portugal!

Yemima: all the way from Mexico, she is especially good at Mexican waves. Yemima's English picked up very quickly during the three weeks; in particular the phrase 'No, I don't think so, Andy', often accompanied by a cheeky grin. Often causing comedy moments, Yemima brought a more international feel to the team.

Jo Wells: 5ft 3in of passion, philosophy and panache. Jo loves sharing her faith and inviting others to meet God. Originally from the south coast but with her university days in Liverpool, she has an interesting accent. Her hobbies include travelling, debating, oh and losing car keys.

Sarah Grimshaw: a kind of Mother Teresa type, who grew up in France as a missionary kid. She has a soft, sensitive nature and a passion for the poor. Fluent in French, Spanish, Portuguese and English, she proved very helpful, frequently digging us out of potential pitfalls.

Ellie Baxendale: heralds from Brierly, near Barnsley. The daughter of a slightly psychotic farmer, Ellie has come through as quite sane. Always offering a thoughtful pearl of wisdom and well up for a laugh, Ellie added a slice of Yorkshire and a touch of class to the team.

Terri Hart: the action girl from Nottingham is in the TA and loves anything physical. Always up for taking on the boys at press-ups, running and general fitness. With her long ginger hair and her endless list of dares, she added a healthy competitive streak to the proceedings.

Becky Fotiou: once described as a walking prayer room, Becky oozes faith and vitality combined with creativity and a beautiful heart. Currently a student at Leeds Uni, she desperately wants to see people know the love of Jesus.

Hannah O'Shea: cool and laid back with her long brown hair, Hannah is the kind of person who talks to you straight. She says it how it is. She is also really fun to try and wind up, occasionally falling hook, line and sinker – monsters in the woods at night, that kind of thing.

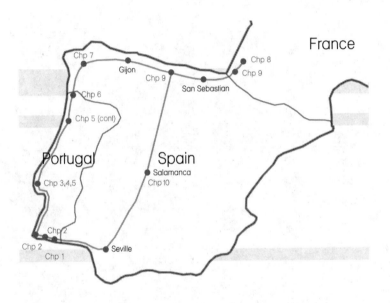

1
And So It Begins . . .

Poring over an open map. Guidebook at the ready. Plane tickets in hand. Rucksack overflowing with boxers. A sense of adventure; anticipating the unexpected; a journey of discovery. New sights. New tastes. New smells. New encounters. . . Experiences that capture the imagination. Ancient ruins. Modern skyscrapers. Postmodern philosophy. Romantic scenarios. . . My heart lives for adventure.

* * *

Reality started to bite as the final family boarded the delayed Easy Jet aeroplane to Portugal with its fabulous orange tint. I began to remember how much I don't like budget airlines.

In front of me a couple of lads were getting the beers in, and as the plane began to shudder along the runway on that hot August day, sweat began to form on my brow. The early morning start and the previous night of frantically packing and fixing surfboards was taking its toll. I felt fidgety and agitated, cramped at the back of the plane, squeezed against the window in a seat not big enough for a child. It always amazes me how charter flights pack us in.

The agitation was bubbling up inside me like a volcano as the beads of sweat began to join up like a dot-to-dot puzzle on my forehead. The tension I could feel across my back was not solely due to embarking on a four-hour flight in a crammed and over-heated, hard-backed plane seat. There was something else troubling my mind.

The summer had already been pretty manic with another Dawn Patrol mission in Cornwall and a diary of preaching engagements. What I really needed by late August was a proper summer holiday, but this was to be no nice end-of-summer vacation.

I looked out of the passenger window and watched as the panels on the wings began to move and the plane accelerated down the runway. What had seemed like a cunning plan in the depths of winter was fast becoming a daunting prospect. Summer missions in the safety of Cornwall were one thing, but my head was swimming with doubts as to what I thought I was doing leading a mission in mainland Europe.

The proposed plan was a road-trip-style mission along the coast of Portugal, Spain and France with a team of young Christians in their late teens and early 20s. This involved jumping in cars and travelling from place to place, working alongside local churches and catching a few waves along the way.

However, what I had planned as being a surf-focused mission was now in some jeopardy, as the team that had been recruited consisted of only two surfers and eleven non-surfers! In many ways I wished it could have been just Jon, the other surfer, and myself. I knew Jon well and we had first met surfing the liquid perfection of Hawaii. We had already travelled extensively together, combining our passion for surfing and mission. Our last trip to Nias had been especially eventful, with earthquakes, famine relief and UN flights home. I hoped this summer would be a little less eventful.

Jon was a good pal and was very much one of those 'wild at heart' types that you could imagine surviving in the jungle quite happily, swinging from tree to tree. The son of missionary parents, he had moved to Indonesia as a kid and grown up surrounded by adventure. A three-week jaunt in Europe wasn't really hard-core enough for Jon – he needed Indians with spears and deadly snakes before he could call something a 'real' mission.

Each team member had applied to come on the trip by filling in an application form. As I had read the forms, I knew that Jon would add his own personal flavour to the mixed bag of individuals. Like an assorted bag of sweets, the team consisted of people with different life stories and experiences that were to become intertwined in the weeks that lay ahead. Eighteen-year-old Terri was from an unchurched family background and hadn't been brought up with religious baggage. She worked in a bar in Nottingham and had come to faith through a Methodist church youth group. In contrast, Ellie had grown up as the daughter of a charismatic Barnsley farmer. Her faith had been grown more gradually and she was presently studying at Durham University.

The variety of backgrounds had intrigued me as I had sat at my office desk months earlier trying to imaginatively construct an Etch-A-Sketch picture of the team in my mind. I looked forward to discovering people's journey of faith so far, and I hoped that through the course of the weeks that lay ahead, each of them would learn to rely more closely upon Jesus.

The main concern that swirled around my mind was people's expectations and how they would interact with one another.

They had paid for their flight and had contributed to the trip and I was unsure as to what they were expecting from this mission experience. This was to be no predictable mission trip and my mind was drowning with nightmare scenarios of conflict as we traversed thousands of miles along the coast.

The mission had been advertised as 'fluid' and 'pioneering', and I hoped that the team would be up for responding to the challenges ahead with that understanding. With no set accommodation sorted for much of the trip and local church contacts that were sketchy to say the least, I knew that we needed to be up for listening to God and following His direction. We needed to move quickly from being a diverse group of individuals to a community that would live by faith, seeking Him for each phase of the adventure. I was also desperate that Road Trip should remain mission and not deteriorate into just three weeks in the sun, drinking margaritas, even though that did sound rather tempting.

As the plane made its way through the clouds and an air hostess charged ridiculous prices for a Cup-a-Soup, I began to pray. The whole Road Trip idea had seemed so right all those months ago and I prayed for God's peace in the depths of my being.

The concept had grown out of a gradual burden that God seemed to be putting on my heart for the bigger picture – for Europe. Several defining moments had brought me to this place and I began to revisit some of those moments in my mind as I felt God's peace kick in.

* * *

One of those defining moments had been the Christian Surfers International Conference in France. I find conferences can sometimes be quite stale, but with an international selection of surfers with the predictable Hawaiian and Aussie delegates and the rather unexpected Japanese and Peruvian contingent, this conference had really come to life. There were lots of stories and sharing of what God was doing in different nations. This, coupled with a big early autumn swell, had made the week really memorable.

But it was the finale of the conference that had been particularly defining in my decision to make this Road Trip. The week had climaxed with a massive beach party with the surf rock band Narrowpath and a Christian Surfers movie premiere, freshly dubbed in French. The night had been a significant piece of outreach, attracting hundreds of surfers who heard the gospel, many of them for the first time.

This finale event had taken place at a beach bar and we had organised to go back to this same bar as part of the Road Trip adventure. The local church we had worked with during the conference was already having half-nights of prayer to gear up for what God was going to do in this south-west corner of France.

I had come back to the UK buzzing with excitement about the doors that were opening up on the mainland. In a prayer meeting in the rolling country hills of the Cotswolds, I had shared my thoughts with Rich. Rich is one of those charismatic characters with wild ginger and bleached hair that sprouts from his head with a passion. His hair somewhat epitomises his passionate nature and his excitable personality. He is a gung-ho crazy surfer, always believing that the biggest swell will hit next week, even when the forecast is that the surf will be flat.

He had a passion for Europe too, and in particular France. He had taken a road trip with friends after finishing Bible college, travelling down the coast of France. He recounted stories of epic waves and caravan fires as we sat perched over a map of Europe, miles from any waves in the Cotswolds conference centre. We began praying for the continent of Europe and in particular the coastline around the three countries. It was from this prayer time that the dream to send mission teams to the mainland began to become a reality.

Rich was to be my partner in crime in scheming the Road Trip concept. We had met, often over a surf, to plot and plan the summer's activities. But somehow I had ended up leading the Spanish and Portuguese leg alone. Rich is married with two kids and the priority to his family meant that I had been deserted for two-thirds of our cunningly concocted Famous Five-esque mission. Rich was now just coming over for the mission in France with reinforcements numbering about 30 young people.

Still on the plane, I nestled into the headrest and closed my eyes. Remembering God's faithfulness and the way in which I believe He had spoken to us was a real comfort, but again the doubts kicked in like a tug of war inside my head. Had we really heard God, or in a surf-obsessed mind had I heard what I wanted to hear? I didn't actually speak any Spanish or Portuguese, and my French was 'ne pas bien'.

As the plane continued to make its way through the clouds, I tried to let the tension out of my shoulders with a circular motion of my neck. My eyelids were becoming heavy and I knew that I needed to get some shut-eye. Within what seemed like moments, the plane was coming in to land.

* * *

When you arrive in a different country, there is always a different aroma. It was a hot and clammy late afternoon and a sweaty smell engulfed my nostrils as we marched out of the baggage reclaim area and into the main entrance of the airport. The area was surprisingly quiet, with only the occasional swathe of holidaymakers with sunburned faces pushing trolleys piled high with suitcases and clutching carrier bags chinking with bottles.

With the five of us packed into the newly acquired hire car and our bags overflowing into the back seat, we began to head away from the airport along the pristine dual carriageway towards Faro. Our eyes worked overtime as they adjusted to the new surroundings set before us: a beautiful city with winding streets, lively bars and a very Mediterranean feel. *The Lonely Planet Guide* described it as 'a real city' with 'considerable charms', although not as 'balmy as other resort towns'.

Somewhat out of character, a McDonald's restaurant sat among the line of old buildings with a rather sinister feel. Though familiarity is always nice, it does seem that wherever you go in the world, the sense of adventure is somewhat diminished by multinational predictability. The McDonald's restaurant and the bountiful supply of cash machines epitomises how easy travelling around the world has become today on these tried and tested routes. We live in a global village where fashion and consumerism are shared through the web of technology.

As an English guy arriving on the mainland of Europe, this is no new feat. Thousands of Brits descend along the coastline every year in pursuit of sun, sex and cheap beer. Yet the relationship between the UK and the mainland of Europe is much older than this explosion of cheap flights and package holidays. There is a rich tapestry of story that sews the countries of Europe together, and it began centuries before a world of fast-food outlets and coffee brands came into being.

This is the story that fascinates me. I am intrigued by these sudden moments when the path of history is diverted and shoots off in a different direction – the stories of significant battles, political movements and cultural shifts that fill our history books. But more than that, I am intrigued by the stories of individuals that pepper history – those individuals who brought about significant change.

Then the spiritual dimension is also intriguing: those God-episodes when people of faith stepped in to shape the nations. The pattern of history is interwoven with ordinary people engaging in God's rescue mission to save the world. Their hero was Jesus and they were His plan.

The sun had now set as we cruised down the narrow streets of Faro and I reflected further on the history of Europe. My mind continued to picture those men and women who had lived out the gospel message across the generations.

The obscure movement that had kicked off in Israel 2,000 years earlier had travelled like an epidemic across the nations. Heroes of the faith like Paul were driven by a passion to see Jesus shared with the Gentiles. Over the 300 years that followed, Christianity grew until the Roman Empire itself became Christianised under Augustine.

As the mighty Roman Empire had gradually diminished, it had been the Celts that had re-evangelised Europe in the depths of the Dark Ages. St Patrick's legacy was thousands of Irish monks choosing to be catapulted into exile for Christ. These monks, with a zeal for the gospel, began planting monastic communities across the continent from Iceland right into the depths of the Germanic people. Tradition has it that some monks got into boats without oars and allowed God to take them to where He wanted. A somewhat different technique to boarding a plane from Gatwick.

Then there had been the volatile years of the Reformation under Luther when he had nailed his 95 Theses to the church door at Wittenburg. The Reformation had rippled across Europe proclaiming grace not works, revolutionising the church. Thousands of people accepted Christ. John Wesley, the great revivalist, was one of those individuals who discovered what it meant to know God's grace as he heard Luther's commentary on Romans. On his adventure he encountered the Moravians, who were flourishing during their 100-year prayer meeting. Wesley, inspired by the small praying community that was sending missionaries throughout the world, later brought revival to the UK.

Throughout the centuries there has been this constant traffic across territorial boundaries as people have carried the message of Jesus from generation to generation, centuries before the arrival of Lonely Planet guides. History holds some amazing stories of passionate Christians living out their faith across the continent. But then there are the horror stories too. Stories of crusades and the slave trade that we prefer to forget.

So here we stood, by our poorly parked Corsa, in our baggy jeans and Etnies. Another generation finding a connection with the mainland. The same gospel that had catapulted St Paul out into Europe to reach the Gentiles was now compelling us to go too.

It was at this point that reality struck. We still had nowhere to stay for the night. Having been turned away from the first motel, which was full, I began to think that booking somewhere rather than blagging it would have been a good plan. With a smirk across his face, the motel manager had pointed out that it was now the height of the holiday season. But through God's grace, by 10.30 pm we had found a place to stay. There was room at this inn, though it meant the five of us who had arrived a day early sharing one dimly lit room with bare beige walls.

* * *

Morning came and we added a VW Transporter to our Corsa for the Road Trip that lay ahead. With the VW Transporter with its nine seats and sliding doors, the Road Trip idea began to feel more like an episode of *The A-Team*. I felt like a Hannibal-type figure but without the plan coming together and the cigar wedged into the corner of my mouth.

Gradually the rest of the team arrived one by one with the predictable number of late arrivals, lost baggage and other fiascos. We gathered in a dimly lit room in a cheap motel with a balcony that overlooked a busy square. The curtain blew gently in the cleansing breeze and I asked each person to share their hopes and fears for the trip that lay ahead.

A variety of thoughts emerged from the mixture of faces around the room. The nervousness could be felt as people began to adjust to their new community and surroundings. Hopes for the trip varied. Some hoped for all-out revival while others hoped they would just take the chances that God gave them to speak of Jesus. There were also a number of fears surrounding people's insecurities as to how God could use them. As I sat there, I felt comforted by the fact that it is in our humility and weakness that He is strong.

Last to speak was Chris – one of those prophetic, arty people. You can never predict what will come out of his mouth next and he speaks with the occasional long pause, choosing his words carefully. His bright white skin and typical Brit-on-holiday apparel, including hunting hat, meant he could quite easily be spotted as a tourist. He shared a passage from Joshua about the twelve stones that had been collected as the twelve tribes entered the Promised Land. Clutching the video camera, he explained to the group that he was to be our cameraman for the trip, making a documentary about twelve ordinary people embarking on an adventure together to evangelise three nations in just three weeks. He went on to expound the significance of the story from Joshua. The twelve stones were to mark the passing of history and he felt that he was there to film a piece of history as twelve young missionaries took their Promised Land.

I was somewhat comforted by Chris's words and our differing stories which were beginning to thread together as we began to find ourselves in God's meta-narrative.

It was time to hand all of our insecurities over to God. We started to pray, and as we did, Chris began filming. He panned and zoomed his PD 150 camera rather inappropriately as we tried to look holy while giving over our concerns to God.

As we sat in the room together, it amazed me to think of how we had come to be there. The story that began with a revolutionary, sandal-wearing Jesus, continues today. The story of His movement spans time and space, unfolding through countless history books. And so the epic adventure of the church continues. As times have changed, styles of celebrating and sharing our faith have adapted, but the message remains the same. Road Trip was to be our unfolding story of ordinary people called to be involved in shaping history. We were simply a group of young people, not too dissimilar from those of previous generations, who had heard the simple call to 'Go'.

* * *

The Lonely Planet Guide to Portugal, Lonely Planet Publications, 2004.

Bruce L. Shelley, *Church History in Plain Language*, Word Publishing, 1995.

2

The Rubber Hits the Road

With the atlas of Europe spread open on my lap, the engine purred into action as the key turned in the ignition. The open atlas was an exclamation mark that said, 'The adventure begins here.' Within moments, we had left the subtle beauty of Faro and were headed for the toll roads. Excited chatter filled the VW Transporter as the chilled sounds of Jack Johnson were dispersed through the seats. With my shades nestled on my nose, I began to adjust to the open road that was to be home for the coming weeks. The air-con kicked in and began filtering a stream of cool air into my face, steadily forcing back the segments of sweat that were forming on my forehead.

Lagos, on the south-west tip of Portugal, was our destination and as we entered the town it was clear why it was known as one of the party capitals of Portugal. The thriving club scene and stunning beaches were a big summer draw and the white-washed resort was brimming with energy. Sun worshippers strolled along the streets with bare chests, and beach cafés were buzzing with life. The whole place was a hive of activity.

We needed a plan of action; to get involved in some structured mission. The trip needed to start in the right way and I couldn't allow it to become merely a jolly jaunt. We also needed to eat, as my rumbling tummy had prompted me. But as we drove past a variety of hotel complexes, I decided that after our first night's experiences in Faro, accommodation needed to be sorted and should be dealt with as a high priority. With a tight budget, I scanned the map for campsites. The team were getting restless. They were cramped in the back of the van between surfboards and rucksacks, and I was starting to get requests for the bathroom.

The cheapest campsite was on the edge of the town and we pulled in alongside the car park barrier to discover an overcrowded dust bowl with makeshift washing lines adorned with swimwear. Awash with families and caravans, the site was rammed at the height of the holiday season. Tents and caravans filled the space. There seemed to be no order and no planning, almost as if the site had been erected in complete darkness. With a look of bewilderment at the chaotic campsite before us, we agreed that tonight we would be camping out on the cliffs.

The sweltering heat was almost overbearing as we wandered down the road towards where the cliff edge abruptly dropped to the secluded picturesque beaches beneath. With a lunch of watermelon and fresh bread, we began to unwind after the journey and soak up some of the ambience of the resort.

Bronzed locals began jumping some 20 feet off the cliff that protruded into the pristine sea, and within a matter of a few minutes we had clambered up the side of the rocky outcrop to join them. A healthy competitive streak saw each of the guys from the team perched on the cliff top calculating where best to jump. One by one, white bodies dropped into the blue depths below. A flurry of white bubbles distorted the colours of the ocean momentarily as each guy was welcomed into the cool sea. Then, one by one, heads emerged with open mouths gasping for air.

Back on the beach, adrenaline-induced smiles illustrated our desire for adventure. I knew it was time that we kicked off something of the missional adventure, which was our reason for being there. The mission was another opportunity to scare ourselves, to push ourselves out of our comfort zones. The half-hour lunch break quickly turned into an hour, and the day was in jeopardy of becoming more of a day off than a day of mission. As we sat hugged tightly around the edge of the cliff, desperate for some shade and not to get sunburned, I began to share the initial challenge.

Before the trip we had crafted some tracts that looked at the idea of life as a road trip. They glimmered in the bright sun as Jo shifted the elastic band off and began to distribute them to each team member. Jo had helped design the tracts, and an air of satisfaction came over her as the team's compliments were fed back. Each team member thumbed through the leaflets, scanning the words. The primary colours of the tracts were fitting for the summer months and we thought they would be ideal for bringing the gospel story to life.

Where language became a barrier, these tracts were to be our tools to share the message of Jesus, but I didn't want this to become a leafleting mission, merely handing out literature. I challenged the group to give out no more than three tracts each in the two hours that lay ahead. The idea was to listen to God, where appropriate to spark conversations, and if applicable to give out a tract. The tracts were only a tool. As Jo finished distributing, she challenged the team to go for it and led us in a short prayer. The mission was about to begin.

As the group dispersed up the steep path towards the town to different locations, Jon, Steve and I headed towards the surf spots in search of members of a fellow tribe with whom we could commune. With the surf flat and a distinct lack of surfers, we entered a bar and enjoyed the cool shade, sipping on cold drinks as the ice danced around the glass. Seeking God for some inspiration and with few surfers around, we attempted conversations with a couple of locals.

We turned to the barmaid, who was cleaning glasses. Within seconds of opening our mouths, I could tell that this wasn't going to work. We offered a couple of opening questions about the locality, to spark some conversation, and a confused look filled both the locals' and our faces. The barmaid's eyebrows peaked up, communicating in an instant that she spoke no English. It was evident that no one spoke English. We were off the tourist route in a back-end bar and with no apparent opening. We gave our tracts to three older Spanish men playing cards on the veranda. They shifted through them with their grubby hands, giving us a nod of appreciation. No conversation followed.

Disappointed with our afternoon, we gathered at the cliff edge alongside the vehicles to find Lisa brimming with excitement. Her great Essex-girl accent described the afternoon's activities in a rapid fire of words that could not wait to get out. Accompanied by Yamima, all the way from Mexico, they had been involved in some great conversations. Their tack had involved praying and then just walking up to strangers on the street and engaging in dialogue.

Lisa's boldness was evident as she began to share: 'We saw these two girls and I just had that kind of feeling that I ought to go and speak to them.' Lisa went on to describe Helena and Katrina, two pretty Portuguese late teens who spoke good English.

They were on holiday in Lagos and when they had asked Lisa what she was up to, she had told them that she was 'on a mission from God'. Only Lisa would come up with something so cheesy.

At this remark, the girls had creased up laughing, in no way hiding their ridicule. Lisa and Yemima had laughed too, trying to hide their embarrassment. Lisa had thought about making a quick exit but had instead hung in there, waiting for the laughter to subside. As their laughs diminished, Lisa had continued, 'But it's true. God wants a relationship with you.' Lisa's words were poignant and the laughter completely stopped. One of the girls looked into Lisa's eyes and began to share, 'Actually, I think there could be more – maybe even a God who cares.'

Lisa went on to share about the God she knew, who was not obsessed by ritual but rather by relationship. The girls listened intently before going on their way. A seed had been sown. Lisa and Yemima were thankful that they had had the courage to push through the humiliation of the laughter, as they had won an opportunity to share. Lisa is not very good at hiding excitement and as she shared the story, there was a bounce in her step and the occasional 'Isn't Jesus great!' thrown in for good measure.

Dave the DJ had had a good afternoon too. He had been on the prowl for somewhere to gig that evening, checking out the music scene in Lagos and collecting a variety of club night fliers. Sarah had accompanied him as 'translator' and Chris had been alongside capturing their afternoon on camera. They had been to a variety of night spots, engaging with different club owners. They planned to return later that night, when the bars and clubs would be buzzing with holidaymakers on a big night out. Dave was optimistic of a possible DJ set. Sarah, who spoke some

Portuguese, explained in greater detail some of the conversations, filling in some of the blanks that Dave had sketched round. As the team gradually grew in number around the vehicles, stories were swapped and emotions shared.

Jo had found it tough. Her honesty was comforting. It was good to know that others had found it difficult too. It hadn't just been the surfers. A natural evangelist with a striking personality, Jo has long brown hair and olive skin – an almost Mediterranean look about her. With her evangelistic gifts and the 'local-esque' appearance, what should have been a breeze had been surprisingly difficult. The whole language barrier and the lack of familiar cultural landmarks meant that all of her natural hooks into conversation had been removed. She explained that there were none of the normal mechanisms to use, no event or local church to invite people to.

The mix of responses was quite overwhelming and people continued to exchange highlights of their first tasters of cross-cultural evangelism while they climbed back into the vehicles. The first attempt at mission had been no disaster, but it had not all been straightforward either. With such a range of personalities, no technique was going to be right for one and all. My head began swimming with thoughts as to how we could make sharing our faith more natural in this alien environment. The chatter gradually subsided and people were left with their own thoughts as the post-sun sleepiness gripped us. A short drive for reflection and we would be making our own campsite for the night.

* * *

The tents were soon pitched on the dramatic cliff tops at St Vincent. The brightly coloured Gore-Tex material looked misplaced in the middle of the moonscape surroundings. The tent fabric was being seriously ruffled by the gusty winds. The team agreed that this spectacular setting on the edge of Europe was much better than the predictable, concrete campsite in the town. The howling wind gave it a rather eerie feel, very different from the hustle and bustle of Lagos.

The team were adapting well and bonding as a unit, each getting used to the housekeeping tasks that needed to be done. I had worried that some members of the team might have been a little unhappy without the hot showers and toilet facilities that make life more comfortable, but they had seized the adventure and were happy sleeping rough on the edge of a stunning coastline.

This location had been a priority for many on the trip. I remember months earlier, as people enquired about the mission, they wanted to know if St Vincent was part of the trip. Pete Greig and Dave Roberts' book, *Red Moon Rising*, had painted an extravagant picture of St Vincent as a place of mystery. It was on these cliff tops that Greig had visualised each nation and prayed for the continent of Europe. In his book, he describes St Vincent as a 'wasteland, which has been battered for thousands of years by the collision of the Atlantic and the Mediterranean seas'. He goes on to explain the history of the site. It had been given its name when the martyr St Vincent died. Grieving monks had carried his body to this place and it had become a place of pilgrimage.

As I reflected on the isolated venue, with the vast expanse of ocean that disappeared off into the horizon, I realised that Road Trip was not just a mission. Road Trip was also a pilgrimage. The journey we were embarking on would be an opportunity to discover some pearls of history as we looked ahead to the future. As we reflected on Greig's vision of a faceless army of young people, we realised that we were, at least in part, the beginning of a fulfilment of that vision.

* * *

I watched as the knife slid delicately through the fresh cod. Hannah and Ellie placed the silvery fish inside the metal grid, which framed the fish like a piece of modern art. I continued to watch, captivated by the fresh food that rested upon a collection of rocks over the burning embers of coal. The lit coal and the steady stream of smoke offered an almost idealistic proceeding to the evening.

The wind was howling, but we had sneaked beneath the radar of the prevailing easterlies and stood sheltered under a sky that was lit up with an explosive concoction of pink and red while the sun made its descent over the horizon. As the sun set, the colours were replaced with a bright moon that reflected like a lantern over the expanse of sea beneath the heights of the cliffs.

As the food was shifted from the BBQ grill to the makeshift plates and then finally into our mouths, and as hands juggled both the paper cup of Portuguese wine and the freshly baked bread, the chatter of voices grew silent, and we fell in awe of the Creator. The night took on an almost biblical perspective as Chris, with his video camera balanced precariously on his lap, reminded us of how Jesus and His disciples had shared fish over an open fire. He put down the video camera and we began to share Communion together.

The whole experience was overwhelming as we stood at the furthest outpost of the European mainland, with the ocean before us reaching out to the Americas and Africa. We stood on what had previously been the furthest point that man believed the world stretched to. It was a place of vision and destiny. A place that pioneers and explorers had sailed past in pursuit of discovering new lands. And now here we stood: 13 ordinary 20-somethings on the edge of a new pioneering adventure, dreaming dreams of what could be and what might happen.

Surfer Jon, with his salt-matted dark hair and his fresh-faced look, began to strum the guitar poised on his knee. The time of worship that ensued was one of those special moments when you dare to believe that maybe, just maybe, you might be on the precipice of history. Our voices sounded into the now dark air proclaiming the state of our hearts. Prayers of brokenness ensued as we surrendered to God and asked that we may know Him more.

'Here I am, Lord; use me' was the prayer that echoed into the night and with that we began to pray from the point where the land meets the sea. We clambered up from our BBQ area and into the powerful winds that were tearing across the unprotected cliff tops. As we staggered against the elements, we began to pray for the nations. As one person began to pray, we infectiously all began calling out to God. It was one of those moments where time seemed to stand still as we prayed for the church across the continents. And then, almost as abruptly as our prayers had begun, we again became silent, our eyes transfixed on the moon that was peaking between clouds that raced in the wind.

As the evening drew to a close, I strolled along the ragged cliff tops, excited by what God was doing in our individual lives. This stretch of coastline was something special. Its simple unspoiled beauty was a striking comparison to the built-up resort of Lagos that seemed an eternity away. Too often my life was spent in the busyness of Lagos rather than in the obscure quietness of St Vincent.

St Aidan sat on a ragged outcrop not too dissimilar from St Vincent more than a thousand years earlier. I picture Aidan as quite a slender character with unkempt hair that blew in the wind. I imagine him with a thoughtful look about him with his eyes transfixed on the battling waves of the ocean. He was an Irish monk, well known for his humility and prudence. He had arrived in the north-east of Britain to found a monastic community. With fellow monks, he laboured to build a collection of wooden shacks that perched on the cliff edge. This was his home on the rugged and untamed tidal island of Lindisfarne, generations ago.

Aidan had based his life on the rhythm of the tides. At high tide the sea engulfs Lindisfarne and leaves the rocky island marooned one and a quarter miles from the shoreline. But then as the tide retreats, a causeway provides a safe passage to the island. As the tide came in, Aidan and his monks practised the spiritual discipline of receiving God's love. And then, as the tide ebbed away, they took to responding to His love in worship and service. Each day when the tide seemed to stand still, they were reminded of the peace that comes in our lives when we have struck the balance between receiving and giving.

Over the thousands of years, the pounding waves of the North Sea had shaped Lindisfarne in the same way that the Atlantic Ocean had crafted St Vincent. And as I stood on the cliff tops of St Vincent, caught up in a cocktail of vision and contemplation, I asked God for a fresh understanding of His love for me. In the busy summer months, my life had been encapsulated in doing rather than being. I had not spent enough time watching the flow of the ocean and allowing God to speak. As Aidan had used Lindisfarne as a fuelling station for his missions into Britain, I now had the opportunity to refuel at St Vincent. I watched the moonlight ripple along the ocean surface. Lindisfarne had not been the destination for Aidan, and St Vincent was not our destination, but from these places we are sent. From these times of revelation, these mountain-top experiences, we need to descend back into the valleys of normality, clutching tightly to all that we have received.

Aidan had been sent to Britain. We had been sent to the nations. His mission strategy had been simple, and so was ours. He had spent time walking the lanes that joined the villages, meeting people and where possible sharing his faith. Road Trip was no new invention. Sure, we were in cars, but in fact, here we were, travelling along the roads of mainland Europe with a similar desire to meet locals and talk about Jesus. Road Trip was to be about walking in the footprints of previous generations, learning from their example: travelling; making pilgrimage; being community; discovering God. History was repeating itself.

* * *

Pete Greig and Dave Roberts, *Red Moon Rising*, Survivor, 2004.

Robert Weston, *Celtic Quest*, Gopher Publishers UK, 2001.

www.allsaintsbrookline.org

www.wikipedia.org

3

A Social Conscience

There are moments when stories collide; when two stories suddenly become intertwined and things change. For a moment in time you find yourself in a chapter of somebody else's story, taking a lead role with little forewarning. That is how it was for Sarah that afternoon when she discovered something new of what the gospel means for the poor.

Watching the needle pierce the skin and the thumb slowly plunge the murky brown formula into the vein, Sarah prayed intently as she watched an addict take a hit before dropping the needle to the ground. Blood spluttered from the open wound, further staining the already speckled garments.

* * *

Two days earlier we had arrived in Lisbon at the home of a family called the Uhlers, a contact that I had got through Christian Surfers. We drove slowly up the narrow path, with crumbling high walls on our left and a row of houses stretching away to the right. With the occasional tree looming over the wall and the sun still high in the sky, the woodland created patterns of shade on the rough terrain of the road ahead.

Navigating our way according to the directions that had been emailed some months previously, we finally arrived at the Uhlers' household. It had a short driveway leading to a beautiful two-storey home with a wooden framework. The house was idyllically marooned by luscious green grass and the odd tree. From the garden, the view overlooked the road onto the rugged landscape that dropped off into the sea a few hundred metres away.

The team were excited to have somewhere to be based for four days and we all looked forward to having some local contacts who could help us to integrate into the local community. We hoped that without the daily routine of finding somewhere to stay, we could capitalise on our time and get stuck into some more effective mission.

As we pulled up the narrow drive, shouts of 'They're here!' bellowed from across the house. The front door was wide open, symbolically proclaiming the ideology of 'open house'.

Having never met the Uhlers face to face, and after some sketchy correspondence, I felt a sudden twinge of nerves in my gut and prayed that this would all work out OK. With vast experience of working with Christians from other clans and other countries, I know that there can often be differences that need to be worked through – certain faux pas, which might be theological, relational or due to some miscommunication of what is expected. But as these thoughts clouded my mind, I momentarily put myself in their position. They probably had similar reservations, yet they had still agreed to open their home to a bunch of strangers.

A warm welcome of firm but polite handshakes and smiles was there to receive us. The garden was already stacked with tents, and the small grassy green resembled a Millets display area. Friends of the family were down visiting and the garden was brimming with excited conversation as Road Trip team members emerged with bent backs out of the vehicles.

Marty and Carey Uhler are keen surfers from the States. They are a stunningly attractive couple with sun-kissed faces, and they simply ooze Jesus. Their hospitality confirmed this as they welcomed us in, not as strangers but as co-pilgrims. They already had other guests, but were always up for hosting mission teams. They also had two teenage surf-obsessed sons who carried much of the same demeanour as their parents. The two sons, with shoulder-length, sun-bleached blond hair and impressive tans, could almost have walked in off the set of *Baywatch*.

The garden became ever busier as we set up camp, and the tent showroom began to look more like the Glastonbury Festival. I took a few moments out to chat in more depth with the Uhlers – to pray with them as they etched out their proposed plan for the days that would follow. We shared our thoughts on their veranda as the sun started its descent and a cool wind rolled in from the direction of the sea.

They were excited to be hosting us and hoped that some of our creativity and passion might enthuse the local group of friends they were discipling. They were in the process of planting a fresh expression of church particularly focused on the local surfing fraternity, and were excited to have us working with them for a short season.

Marty's openness in the way he shared put me at ease. Our stories were to meet for a moment and I had the impression that God was going to teach us both new things. He was willing to change the schedule and fit in with our plans, and this willingness to adapt conveyed so much.

The team began to mix with new-found friends over bowls of

chilli. Jon was off watching surf movies with the Uhlers' sons in the side room, and with the TV as background noise they were retelling stories of epic waves. Hannah and Becky were helping out in the kitchen. Ellie and Dave were in deep dialogue with a family of missionaries based in the Netherlands and I could hear Yamima's laugh erupting from the far side of the room. Everyone was quickly integrating.

As the chilli was pumped out from the kitchen, almost like a continuous pipeline of deep-sea oil, people continued to arrive and the noise level in the home quickly rose. Lots of locals were excited to meet us and hear about our trip so far. One of the girls, Jasmin, who was in a punk band, had connected with Jo a year earlier during a missions trip in London. The connection had never been followed up, but unbeknown to Jo, Jasmin was a good friend of the Uhlers. Jo almost burst with excitement as Jasmin arrived. The scream of 'Oh my goodness!' shook the very foundations of the house, maybe even the foundations of Lisbon. A story had reconnected.

As empty bowls and glasses were collected, we gathered together in the lounge. The open-plan room had simple and relaxed décor. It was packed out as people grabbed floor space and jostled till they were comfortable.

Marty, as a gifted worship leader, together with Jon, began to focus the group with a time of sung worship. He started strumming and opened up with an almost poetic prayer. As soon as we began to sing, I had that tingling sensation that God was there. From an array of conversations, our focus was abruptly brought back to Jesus and in the midst of song, a jumping jack of prayers for Portugal swept across the room. The atmosphere was electric and a spiritual connection among strangers formed as we prayed for the locality. An excitement was brewing.

As I scanned the room, taking a moment to log each person's face, it seemed incredible that in this house we had all come from such different places. Different countries. Different church backgrounds. And yet that night our different stories had momentarily become one.

A quick round of introductions followed, with snippets of story and moments of laughter. The Uhlers were from the US and they went on to share their long-term vision amid good-mannered interruptions as people chipped in their thoughts. The Uhlers were passionate church planters and had felt the call to Europe some years earlier. They were real pioneers and had been involved in a variety of mission and church contexts. As they shared, they emanated a humble kind of wisdom that gave me a deep respect for them – I wanted my life to be an adventure like theirs had been.

As we moved from vision to practicalities, the overview for the next few days was shared. We began to pray for specifics, looking forward to all that God had in store. The next day we would be serving an orphanage and teaching them how to surf. I could tell that the Uhlers were slightly disappointed that only Jon and myself were confident enough surfers to teach, but the team stepped up to say that they would lead some other activities on the beach – some wide games to keep the spectators amused.

* * *

Early the next morning and with bleary eyes, we drove the short distance to the beach and looked down at the view from the cliff. A small swell crashed into the wide expanse of yellow sand. The rocky descent was tricky as we struggled down clutching several surf shops' worth of equipment. An array of boards and wetsuits had been sourced earlier that morning from the darkness of the garage beneath the house. The wetsuits had definitely seen better days, but they had been loaded into the back of the truck and a selection of surfboards from different decades had been hoisted on top of the Jeep-type carrier and strapped to the roof. Transporting them down the cliff by hand was the difficult bit.

Once on the beach, we waited for the kids from the orphanage to arrive. I don't quite know what I expected when I heard the word 'orphanage'. I guess I pictured a cast of children straight out of Dickens' *Oliver Twist* – complete with cockney accents and flat caps. It's funny how words can be so loaded and how quickly we can make assumptions.

One of the things that I struggle with about myself is the way I so easily judge and compartmentalise people, especially strangers. From the second I see someone, my mind begins to work overtime, drawing conclusions about who they are and their relative worth. I do it all the time: at the checkout at Tesco's; walking past the old man waiting at the bus stop or past the teenage girl pushing a pram.

I often pray that I would see them as Jesus sees them; that I would see His love for the 'walk-on' characters in my life story because that was what Jesus was all about. Only when we grasp His love for others can we truly begin to recognise that God wants to speak into their lives and that we might be the tool with which He is choosing to do this.

As the orphans made their descent to the beach, I tried to see them through Jesus' eyes. As they got closer, I could see that they looked like any other group of young people. They wore ordinary beach clothes and they were full of excited and possibly slightly nervous chatter as they spilled onto the beach, ready to learn to surf. But I was quickly reminded of how looks can be deceiving.

The two ladies who had brought them to the beach asked us not to take photographs because many of the young people had been abused and were in hiding from parents. Some of the young people had been abandoned – unloved and dumped by family members. Others had lost their parents and had no one else to look after them.

I began to wonder what that must do to a person. To suddenly be left all alone at such a young age. What could the idea of Father God mean to them? What a privilege it was to show them something of Christ's love.

* * *

The team quickly swung into action and through the help of an interpreter began setting up for 'capture the flag'. Meanwhile, others in the group were kitted out in wetsuits and given preliminary warm-up exercises to carry out.

The waves weren't too big, maybe a two- to three-foot face, but the current was strong. The dark sandy beach and the selection of seaweed made the messy conditions seem almost like a soup of unpredictability. The dumping waves crashed against the shoreline, pulling violently in different directions as the wash and the backwash collided in mid-flow. These were not ideal conditions.

The first girl I was to teach was about 13 years old. The wetsuit hugged her small frame as she lugged the surfboard to where I stood. After a brief safety overview, the lesson began. We waded in waist deep and she gradually adjusted to the frosty reception of the cold water. She was clinging on tightly with white knuckles, and as the next wave came I pushed the board headlong towards the shore. Wipe-out. The board had caught an edge and she was thrown into the shallow waters and pounded by the might of the wave.

I quickly strode over towards the board and pulled her to the surface. She had been under for a few seconds – long enough to give someone a scare. As I pulled her to the surface, she had her fingers pinched over her nose and her eyes squeezed tightly shut. Her fear was evident. She had tucked up into a tight ball in fear rather than try to get to the surface in the waist-deep water.

As the panic began to retreat from her face, I tried to explain that she needed to try to stand on her feet. She spoke no English, so I tried to communicate with brash actions and a foreign accent. It had seemed like a good idea in my head, but she just looked at me strangely.

Before long, she had ridden a couple of waves and had done well. She looked exhausted but satisfied, and when I motioned to her to go back to the beach, she readily accepted the offer, heading straight back to grab a towel.

The games were continuing. The perfectly flat beach had now been turfed up as bare feet chased up and down the sand. I could see that the fitness of the team was somewhat lacking, as they were being outpaced continually by the orphans.

Local surfers, local Christians, the orphans and our road trippers interspersed, sharing stories about the morning's activities. Conversations in broken English continued over the packed lunch. The leaders of the orphanage were really grateful and the Uhlers promised future excursions. It had been such a simple operation and we had shown them something of Christ in the way that we had made ourselves available; in the way that we had served; in the way that we had loved.

* * *

Earlier in the summer, near to Lisbon, one of the top beaches for locals to spend the hot summer days had been raided by a large number of young people. They had systematically worked their way across the beach, mugging each and every group of people. Wallets, watches and mobile phones were swiped and there had been an element of fear ever since.

The Uhlers had decided that it would be a good idea to go and systematically bless the beach. So, with a quick stop at the supermarket, they arrived carrying bags of water and cake to distribute free of charge to locals who were enjoying the hot sun and the sea breeze. As distribution began, the team prayed across the beach, and slightly hesitant and suspicious sunbathers began to accept these free gifts.

As the afternoon ventured on, the team found themselves dispersed, conversing with different individuals in very different circumstances. Yemima was very excited to find a Spanish guy on holiday. Being from Mexico, she had missed conversing in her own language and here was her opportunity. He was perched on the beach, enjoying the water and cake, slightly confused by the fact that it was free. She immediately burst into sharing the gospel in her native tongue as Lisa prayed from the sidelines.

Lisa couldn't understand the course of the conversation that was developing and she instead began to listen to God. As the conversation between Yemima and her new-found friend reached a lull, Lisa caught Yemima's attention.

'I think God's saying that this guy is very unhappy in his job, that he is washing cars or something . . . something that seems very insignificant. And I feel that God wants to tell him that He is there with him . . . and that He loves him no matter what job he does.'

Yemima began to laugh. 'This is what we have just spoken about! This guy hates his job and feels very insignificant.' As a stunned Yemima turned to her new-found friend and shared Lisa's words, the conversation reignited as a stunned Spanish guy agreed to receive prayer.

Dave and Steve somehow ended up helping some bricklayers lay bricks. The offer of bottled water on the steaming hot day had been welcome. As one of the brickies chugged the water, it dribbled down his sweaty muscular torso. Steve had then decided to give the bricklayers a hand, so he took off his t-shirt and lifted the coarse bricks in his sweaty hands. The bricklayers were somewhat bemused. Maybe Steve wanted a job.

Sarah and Jon were escorted by a local Christian girl called Maia to a very different world. They were on an estate just a stone's throw from the beach. This was an alien context compared to that of the beach. The slum was a place known for drug addiction and prostitution, and was not on the tourist route! Armed with bottles of water, cake and prayer, they began to meet some of the inhabitants. Sarah immediately began to pray, not against the flesh and blood, but against the strongholds that gripped this deprived area – an area that had been forgotten by the world and the sunbathers relaxing moments away.

Sarah prayed intently as a tall dark guy got out of his car and started walking in her direction. He had been exchanging packages for money from the driver's seat. She prayed for him as he strode past. The dark lines under his eyes and his haunting face were a picture of brokenness. Sarah lowered her head to hide the tears as she continued to give out bottles of water.

As the syringe dropped to the floor, she held out a bottle of water to the lady whose ragged clothes were stained a dirty blood brown from years of injecting. Sarah had an overwhelming urge to hug the lady, who looked drained of life. But Sarah pulled back as she fought the tears. Later she would regret not holding that lady even for a moment, but no one would blame her.

Sarah and the woman were metres away from each other, but their stories were oceans apart. It is amazing how these very different women, with two very different stories, could very easily have remained unassociated for a lifetime. But in an instant their lives collided. Sarah, with her graduate degree, had a lifetime of opportunity ahead. This lady, with a glazed look in her eyes, had few prospects. Sarah had a future, but all the woman appeared to have was a past. God loves them both.

Life is full of colliding stories and, with just the briefest of interactions, there is the possibility for change. Seeing true poverty with your own eyes can change a person. As Sarah encountered the drug-induced desperation in those individuals, children continued to play around the streets. As she engaged with what was happening, she sensed something of the call of God. Was He calling her to care for the forgotten estates of Europe? Those forgotten places where people live lives of desperation just a short distance from the beaches of her middle-class normality?

William Booth had seen first hand the kind of suffering that existed in the world. He had grown up in Nottingham and received an apprenticeship with a pawnbroker at the age of 13. He saw the misery and hardship that allowed the pawnbrokers to flourish. When his father died a year later, he tasted poverty himself.

He lived in the mid-nineteenth century and moved to London in a time when cities were blossoming in the thick smoke of the Industrial Revolution. Countryside residents were enticed by the towering chimneys and opportunity for riches.

Booth was a slight man with a long snaking beard, an auto-cratic kind of leader with a preaching style that drew the masses. He believed that to improve the condition of the 'wretched' he had to get at their hearts. Social transformation began with transformation of the heart.

So he founded the Salvation Army, an evangelistic movement with a strong social conscience. He was seen by many as a threat: a threat to the church hierarchy, because it failed to connect with the masses; a threat to brewers and pimps, with business being eroded by the rapid growth of the Salvation Army. Booth often provoked reaction as he encouraged his disciples to sing temper-ance songs near pubs. Frequently, violent clashes ensued. But greater than that, he posed a threat to poverty.

Alongside W. T. Stead, a leading journalist, and Frank Smith, Booth set up a number of social reforms. With their shared think-ing, they wrote *In Darkest England and The Way Out*, a bestseller that argued that the poorest tenth of the population in England were as much in slavery as certain African tribes. The Salvation Army became synonymous with social reform as they cam-paigned for change and put the book's ideology into practice. They set up a labour bureau; a missing person's bureau; a farm to teach agricultural skills; and they established businesses, including a match factory and a tea packaging warehouse to model good employment practice. More controversially, Stead bought a girl called Eliza out of prostitution in London, for five pounds, to raise awareness of child prostitution.

The church had boomed in the first centuries of the first mil-lennium as Christians had shown Jesus through sacrificial care for the poor. History documents the stories of early Christians who remained with the sick when plagues ravished cities, jeopardising their own health, as everyone else fled. Centuries later, Booth had rediscovered that the gospel preached should be shared with the gospel lived. He had been given a passion for the poor and as Sarah continued to share her story with the group, we were challenged to remember that call to serve the poor. God loves the poor. God loves justice. But the question is, do we?

* * *

Stephen Brook, *God's Army*, Channel 4 Books, 1998.

Tim Dowley, *The History of Christianity*, Lion Publishing, 1990.

Rodney Stark, *The Rise of Christianity*, Harper (San Francisco), 1997.

4

Jesus in a Night-Club

'Sharing your faith in night-clubs?' A dubious look fell over the young Portuguese man's face. Named David, he traded trainers in Barcelona, but had returned to the Uhlers' in Lisbon to join us for the Portuguese leg of Road Trip. This wasn't his idea of mission activity.

Remaining rather sceptical, he agreed to take us into town. He still believed that this was a ploy to go and party. He couldn't understand the concept of mission in bars and night-clubs. This was where people went to 'sin'. The team had bombarded him with Bible stories of Jesus with the prostitutes, the tax collectors and the sick, but he just offered a cheeky smirk by way of response.

He promised us a short drive 'round the corner', but something must have been lost in translation because the short drive took a clear hour. However, the mood remained upbeat in the van as we sang along to the 80s classics that were pumping from the local Portuguese radio station.

As we made our way through the network of narrow lanes in the heart of Lisbon, we finally pulled into a dimly lit car park. I parked the van alongside David's car and one by one the team piled out of the vehicles and began to form a huddle. Our Portuguese friend was still to be convinced that this was mission.

As we gathered in the huddle, I felt it was time to give one of those startling speeches that you always see in the epics like *Spartacus* before your comrades in arms march off towards the front line. Chris had his camera poised to capture my sterling charge, but my bumbling words were less like Spartacus and more like Simpson. With that began a time of prayer. Short prayers popped out of the huddle like popcorn in a pan. Prayers for miracles; prayers for boldness; prayers for good conversations.

As the group stood there huddled in this dark car park praying, passing strangers glanced curiously as they wandered past. As the prayers went on, a greater passion was fuelled and to conclude the time of prayer, a mighty 'Amen' exploded from the group, echoing around the old derelict buildings that surrounded the car park. We turned to face the strip of neon lights that shone in the darkness, offering a warm sinister glow.

The plan of action was quite simple: we would divide into two groups, pray down the strip of clubs and see where we felt God was leading us. We would then enter one of the fine establishments, buy a drink and start conversations about Jesus. We were asking that God would prompt us as to where to go and who to speak to. This was going to be the kind of night where we had to keep listening and following His lead.

Some of the group felt really comfortable in this situation. Becky and Hannah were real club babes and liked this style of evangelism. This was an average night out in studentdom – hitting the clubs to worship God, pray and look for openings to share.

Dave too was pretty confident, yet humble at the same time.

He strode towards the strip of clubs, chattering away. As a DJ, the club scene was his home and he aimed to spend the night mingling with club promoters to try and blag a gig for another night. CDs of his mixes had been sent out a month previously to the Portuguese contacts, but they had remained unsure as to what kind of club we were after and had failed to secure a venue. This didn't deter Dave and though he would never do this in the UK, rocking up to clubs and asking for a gig, this was Portugal and he may never come here again. He had no shame.

Some of the team had never done this before and I felt that as team leader and evangelist, I should show them how it was done. It felt as if their eyes were fixed on me as the old wise guru of clubbing mission (even though I had stopped going regularly over the past five years). I strode comfortably down the strip of bars and clubs, walking in the glow of the lights. Prayers escaped under my breath and I tried earnestly to listen to God and hear His voice clearly.

Whenever I come to listen to God, I always struggle with discerning whether I am hearing Him or whether my own thoughts are emerging. I felt pressurised to hear God, as I knew that the night had the potential to go a little pear-shaped. Our Portuguese contact was still convinced that we were out to party, and to make the two-hour round trip worthwhile, we needed some godly inspiration!

As the two groups parted, I led my contingent further down the strip, with different sounds and smells pouring out of each venue. There was a rich mix of drinking arenas, ranging from the swanky bar with blocks of primary colour decking the walls, to the more old school, authentic-looking pub with stools and pints of Guinness. As we continued along the strip, we eventually settled on a modern-looking bar. The bright silver metal-framed tables and chairs positioned outside in the warm late evening air attracted most of our group, but I ventured on inside the bar. With my hand searching frantically around the inside of my jeans pocket to find the correct change, I ordered drinks for Becky and myself. As the drinks were poured, I started scanning the bar for someone to talk to and share my faith with.

The bar was long and thin, with a pool table perched at the back that was swarmed by would-be players waiting for their chance on the table. Occasional streams of smoke rose towards the high ceiling as people lit up, and a murmur of chatter filled the air.

Spotting an empty table, I wandered over with Becky and we sat on the sidelines, people watching and trying to get a grasp of what was what. About 15 minutes later, I began to get impatient and after what seemed like an eternity glancing around the bar, I decided to try and launch into a conversation with a group on the next table. There were seven people crowded around two tables that had been pulled neatly together. A selection of half-empty drinks sat on the table and there was little conversation. I couldn't quite work out their relationship to one another. They were made up of a broad spectrum of ages ranging from a pretty brunette 20-something to a grey-haired, stereotypically Portuguese-looking man in his late 50s. They looked friendly enough and I shuffled my chair towards them and lent in.

I decided to go for the tried and tested conversation opener, asking about the local nightlife and the best spots to visit, starting off, of course, with the classic line, 'Excuse me – do you speak English?'

As the conversation began to flow, more like a trickle than a deluge, and as the table rather unenthusiastically told me about the local bars, I realised that I had made a grave error. This was not just any bar. This was a karaoke bar! The realisation hit me as someone began to sing with incredible gusto the theme tune to *The Titanic*.

Conversation became very difficult as the music deafened everyone in the bar. The occupants of the tables I had shuffled towards made little attempt to make me feel welcome any longer. With their short snappy responses, I got the impression that they did not want to move on to a conversation about the meaning of life. Perhaps it was the fact that I didn't speak any Portuguese. Perhaps they thought I was cracking on to the 40-year-old lady who was wearing a rather fetching red top and appeared to be the one without a partner for the night. Perhaps they just loved karaoke.

I turned back to my table and, rather humbled by my first attempt, decided that more prayer might be a good plan of action. I quietly prayed for those I had spoken to and scanned the room again for others to share with. Becky, who had now almost finished her drink, was desperate to hit a different bar where she could get dancing. She asked me for the plan. With little idea of what to do next, I shrugged my shoulders and leaned back into the chair.

I decided to go right in for another conversation with a guy on a different neighbouring table. My impatience shining through, I used a different tack and asked him how the whole karaoke thing worked. He looked like an intense disco diva with his top shirt button undone and his thick brown chest hair wavering out of the top. His haircut was something reminiscent of Elvis. He spoke English, which was a great relief, but the shortness of his answers revealed that he did not want to move into deeper conversation either. He was quite clearly there for the karaoke and didn't want to be distracted by an Englishman or, worse, a karaoke novice.

Once again I leaned back into the safety of my chair, which

symbolically defined my comfort zone. The night wasn't going to plan. I thought of the rest of the team stationed outside, and hoped that they were having greater success. As I began to reflect on the night so far and what to do next, the bar erupted in cheers as the next karaoke volunteer strode into the centre of the venue and, with mic in hand, began some crazy dance routine, shaking his rear end like a Brazilian carnival dancer. As the bar, which was getting ever more crowded, whooped at his dancing magic, I wondered quite what I had got myself into.

As the night drew on, I began to work out what we should do next. It struck me how wild the bar went when a new karaoke singer stepped into the breach and it suddenly occurred to me that it might be a good idea for one of the team to give the old singing a go. I thought of Jon and his voice. If people go wild at a man moving his ass, Jon would surely wow the crowd with his infectious rendition of 'Lady in Red'.

I moved over to the control desk and slid Jon's name and song title along to the guy in charge. Rather than trying to initiate conversations, perhaps Jon's captivating performance would draw people to us. Jesus told stories; Jon could sing karaoke. It made perfect sense. The karaoke organiser lifted the slip of paper towards his eyes and then smiled back at me. It was now time to tell Jon his fate!

Having set Jon up beautifully, I was quite pleased when the next singer was somewhat worse. It meant Jon had little competition. I decided to leave the rest of my group as Jon came to terms with his destiny. The strip of bars was now busier than ever and again I began to pray. The night seemed to have been very ordinary, and tiredness had begun to envelop me.

Questions buzzed around my head as to what God wanted us here for. Maybe we should change tack, giving out tracts and then legging it rather than shooting for in-depth dialogue? I had put myself out on a couple of occasions, but there had been no open doors. I began to reconcile myself to the thought that perhaps we were here just to pray.

I met up with DJ Dave, who had been checking out the scene in a variety of clubs. As we walked down the strip, Becky joined us and the boom of the bass drew us into a rather secluded night-spot, set back off the main path. We navigated our way past the bouncer and made our way towards the DJ stand, where Dave was to see if he could score a set for the next night. He was then introduced to the bar manager while Becky and I waited on the dance floor and began to worship and pray as the bass line kicked in.

A variety of people in their 20s and 30s were moving in rhythm as the beat came to a crescendo. Like a hive of bees around a honey pot, packs of hungry men swarmed around groups of dolled-up girls coated in make-up. And there, on the edge of the dance floor, we danced and interceded for this generation of Portuguese young adults who seemed to be lost in a euphoria of indulgence.

'It's almost time,' said Becky with over-exaggerated movements of her mouth, while pointing at her watch. We left the club and found seats on the decking further down the strip where we had agreed to reconvene with the team.

Feeling rather disappointed with how the evening was going, I lay back in the chair and began to psyche myself up for the journey home. While pondering the thought of another long drive, a couple of men strode up to me in need of a cigarette lighter. I told them that I had no lighter and then, rather surprisingly and without asking, they drew seats alongside me and asked what we were doing here tonight.

At this point my heart jumped as I began to excitedly share in a mixture of French, English and somehow Portuguese that we were Christians praying and talking about Jesus. A quick 'thank you, Lord' flared heavenwards as the men tried to comprehend what I was saying. Both were in their late 20s and were dressed to impress, with neatly ironed shirts and a distinct smell of expensive aftershave. The guy sitting next to me appeared the more confident of the pair and began to ask exactly what I believed.

As I engaged in conversation, others on the team began to reconvene and gather around his friend, who was soon also conversing about Jesus. As the conversation progressed, it emerged that the guy I was talking to was a backslidden Christian. Condemned by his local church for drinking and smoking, he had given up on his faith. He told me of the hurt and pain he had felt as he was asked not to return on Sunday mornings. The church didn't want a bad reputation. His pain was obvious and it was clear that he was still searching for the peace of God in his life.

I chatted through the gospel and apologised for how we as the church often judge rather than show grace. Tears began to well up in his eyes as I told him that God still loved him and wanted a relationship with him. He had been shocked that we were out in the clubs of Lisbon 'on mission', and when we offered to pray for him there and then, he looked quite bemused. But he accepted, and some of the group laid their hands on the two guys and prayed that they might know God more fully. In the midst of a strip of clubs, as people continued to walk noisily past, and as a variety of music genres blared into the night sky, God was at work.

* * *

I have found that few people in the church like the concept of mission. We try and do our bit after a particularly convicting sermon. Maybe we have friends round for a coffee and, in polite conversation, share a snippet of testimony. Or perhaps we push an invitation to an Alpha supper into the hand of a work colleague with a reddening face and flurry of words that sounded so much better in our head. But the challenge to go into the uncomfortable places to share the gospel, well, that is kind of awkward.

William Carey is one of my heroes. He seems to have been quite an ordinary bloke. An ordinary bloke who had a passion for the lost. He was the son of a weaver, and being a sickly child meant that he became a shoemaker. When he read the gospels through, his simple faith and the reality of the teaching of Jesus convinced him that he needed to 'go into all the world' and he decided he would become a missionary to India.

But in the eighteenth century, the church didn't agree. The church taught that there were certain places where Christians should not go. One morning Carey expressed his desire to go to India while speaking at church. He shared his desire to reach the unreached people groups. As he shared his thoughts, a minister is said to have exclaimed, 'Young man, sit down. When God pleases to convert the heathen, he will do it without your aid or mine.'

Undeterred, Carey set off for India and dedicated his life to building an indigenous church where Jesus was at the centre of the existing culture. He did not wish to import Western substitutes but to build a culturally sensitive Christian community among the people.

Jesus died for the people of India. Jesus also died for the clubbers of Portugal. If we live in fear of taking the message to the masses into the uncomfortable places, we will miss the opportunity of being Jesus to entire swathes of people. We must take precautions. We must pray. But we must never hide away from our duty to go into 'all the world'. As Carey built an indigenous church in India, part of my generation's call is to build an indigenous church community for the generation of clubbers. The clubbers who were dispersing into the cooler night air of Lisbon.

As we embarked on the journey back, it turned out that Jon had miraculously escaped singing at the karaoke bar. We laughed about the night's events and then gradually left each other alone with our thoughts.

David sat apprehensively next to me, rethinking his views on mission. 'So you go to clubs quite a lot to talk about Jesus, Andy?' he questioned. With a slight smile, I simply said that I wanted to go where I thought Jesus would go. Hitting the clubs was not as pioneering as we had been taught to believe. People like Carey had been taking the gospel to the lost for centuries. David returned to his thoughts as he gazed out of the window into the night sky.

'Personally,' I said, 'I reckon Jesus would have been a clubber.'

* * *

Ruth Tucker, *From Jerusalem to Irian Jaya*, Zondervan, 2004.

5

The Italian Job

With a final day left in Lisbon and no set plan, some sight-seeing seemed to be in order. A spectrum of offers was laid on the table and David was keen to show off some of the local historical treasures. We decided that Sintra Castle, perched in the hilltops just north of Lisbon, would be our destination.

The slow drive along the narrow roads that zigzagged up the hillside created a sense of adventure as the view of Lisbon beneath ever increased with every turn in the road. The castle punctuated the skyline with a series of turrets that protruded from the green tree tops and holly.

The castle was built by the Moors in the eighth and ninth centuries on solid boulders of rock, and for centuries had provided a cooler location for the aristocracy to escape the hot sun and enjoy the mountain breeze. From the car park, a forested path followed the base of the castle walls, until a crumbled section allowed visitors to enter beyond the periphery and up into the ancient corridors of the grey and white stones that have remained cemented together for many a lifetime.

The Moors were nomadic people from North Africa, chiefly of

Berber and Arabian stock. In the eighth century they had been converted to Islam and their invasion of mainland Europe had shaped the landscape incalculably, with their universities, their architecture and their farming techniques. The Moor Empire that had once stretched beyond the Pyrenees and into France was now gone and this castle was one of the retreating memories of a bygone era.

It is amazing to think of the civilisations that built these castles without the modern machinery we rely on today. The meticulously constructed maze of turrets was bordered by the perfect blue sky as we ascended and then descended series of steep staircases and narrow paths that hugged the outer walls of the castle. The walls then cascaded down sheer drops to the rocky outcrops below. The contrast of colour and texture was truly extraordinary as big bold smooth boulders of white rock, ancient grey castle walls and the patchwork of bright greenery collided to create a veritable kaleidoscope. The castle is an old ruin, a shadow of its former glory and from the top flies the brightly coloured green and red of the Portuguese flag.

From the pinnacle tower, we looked back on the winding stone steps that meandered behind us. A captivating view stretched into the distance as forest greens eventually reached urban dwellings in the distance. Having finally ventured to the very top of the fort, there was a feeling of accomplishment from the panoramic ascent.

As I subtly tried to get my breath back, I began to picture the past. I began imagining the battles that had taken place as the Moors were pushed out of this castle and out of Western Europe. While the Muslim Moors left from the West, Pope Urban II (in 1095) was mobilising an army of thousands of soldiers to win back Jerusalem from the Muslim Turks to the East. Classified as a 'holy war', blessed by the church, an army made up of a united Europe moved onto the offensive and attacked the Islamic strongholds with a series of Crusades that have bloodied the church in history books ever since; Crusades that aggressively killed rather than lovingly converted.

When conversing with friends about the gospel of love, people have often asked, 'But what about the Crusades?' I find it hard to apologise for something in which I took no part, like a German apologising for the war. But although it seems a little contrite, I always try to apologise for the church's bad history. If I want to celebrate the great aspects of our Christian heritage, I must be willing to accept some of the collective responsibility for the evil that has been done in the name of Jesus. When it comes to the church, people take notice if we stop being proud and admit that we have got things wrong. So this heartfelt 'sorry' is what I give. I just hope that, generations down the line, my ancestors aren't embarrassed by the things that we do. I hope that they don't have to offer difficult apologies for our shortcomings.

As generations before had come with swords, we came with prayer, and to remind the group that we were still on mission, I thought that this would be a great place to pray – to maintain our focus on Jesus. The rugged rock had an almost box-shape chamber that offered postcard perfect views in every direction.

'What a great place to pray,' I exclaimed as the warm breeze filtered through our huddle of friends absorbing the view, filing each detail away in memory banks for when we were back in the gloomy British winter.

'How about we pray for Portugal from this high ground?' Nods of enthusiasm abounded.

'And how about we pray out loud?' The nods were slightly less enthusiastic.

Really getting into the idea, I suggested, 'And what about doing it Korean style, so that some of us sing a worship song while the rest of us pray?' The nods stopped.

I wanted our faith to be more obvious. So often we hide away in our church meetings and home groups, keeping our spiritual life hidden from the world. We had been reading through Acts each morning as a team and the concept of a visible Christian community had kept being impressed upon me.

Throughout the Road Trip we had been reading our Bibles in public places – in coffee shops, in bars and on beaches. However, praying and worshipping out loud was definitely one step further outside of our comfort zone.

Reluctantly the team gathered to face the south and we rattled through a number of things we thought would be good to pray for, in particular some of the specifics that we sensed God was saying about the trip and about Portugal.

Jo began to sing as we turned to look beyond the walls. 'Holy, holy, holy' drifted around the watchtower as she gained confidence in her act of worship. A trickle of prayers began to flow from the team members' mouths. Some of the tourists looked up in surprise and some decided it was time to leave. Undeterred, though ever conscious of what was going on, we continued our public spectacle. One group of tourists stayed, captivated by the proceedings. Though they did not understand what was being sung or spoken, they understood the heart of its meaning. Clapping softly to encourage us on, we moved to face the east.

A couple of the team were 'not into this' and quietly bowed their heads, at the same time keeping an eye on the other tourists' reaction to our obscure prayer practices. They offered a quiet prayer while trying not to be overly associated with the rest of the group. As we continued to pray, our prayers reached a humble crescendo and then gradually we fell silent before turning our attention to the west. Again there was a humdrum of prayer that seemed to drift almost magically from this high point before descending abruptly down and over the forest below. Prayers for the broken. Prayers for the hurting. Prayers for the lost. Prayers for the drug addicts. Prayers for the unloved children.

As the spoken prayers began to quieten again, we turned to the north, but our out-of-place behaviour had caused somewhat of a stir, and a group of young Italian men began to ask what we were up to. As discussion began, I stepped back to continue to pray. Hannah, Lisa and Ellie began to engage in quiet conversation, sharing about prayer.

The Italians had had bad experiences of the church. They argued that religion was created by men in power to control the masses. Religion for them was about sets of rules that programme us to live subdued lives with the hope of one day getting to paradise. They reckoned that if there was a God, he definitely was not of the personal sort. Hannah was in a perfect place to be able to begin to answer some of their questions. She too had grown up a Catholic and she too had thought that Christianity was a legalistic religion. Her radical conversion story about discovering a relationship with God provoked further discussion, though the Italians remained sceptical. Lisa was on hand to give them tracts as our prayer fest came to a conclusion and we went our different ways.

As we began to descend from the top of the castle, I was struck by the thought that we often forget that we are on a mission. Not just on this Road Trip, but every day of our lives. We too readily forget that every day there is an opportunity for something extraordinary to happen. Instead we go about life never expecting God to give us a divine meeting.

On the way down the narrow paths, Hannah began to share in more depth about the conversation. The Italians were searching for a real spirituality and their biggest hang-up was their experience of church. How true this is for our generation that is intrigued by Jesus but too often turned off by churches that appear to be archaic legalistic establishments. Church needs to be about our relationship with God and experiencing His Spirit. The Italians were on a road trip of their own, seeking to enjoy time journeying and exploring. They had a similar heart for adventure and pilgrimage, but without Jesus.

As we reached the van and began our journey back to the Uhlers', a feeling of regret began to fill Lisa, Jo and Hannah. God had given us this opportunity to share our faith, but we had not prayed for the Italians. Jo in particular was angry at herself for not offering to pray. She was pretty gutted, and in her repentance she prayed for our new-found Italian friends whom we would probably never see again, that they might discover Jesus.

That night we prayed for them again. And the following morning too. God seemed to have put them on a number of people's hearts. Corporately we prayed that as they journeyed along the coastline, they might be put in the path of other Christians. Feeling as though we had let God down we also prayed that we would have the confidence to seize future opportunities to pray with others.

* * *

After a time of breakfast and prayer (and another quick surf in some quality six-foot face and glassy waves for Jon and me), we said goodbye to the Uhlers and their other guests. The tents were packed away and big hugs were shared all round rather than the polite handshakes we had opted for on our arrival.

It is amazing how deep relationships can be formed in such a limited time and as the bags were loaded into the VW, we spent time praying for the Uhler family. It felt like an incident right out of the New Testament as we blessed their family and their ministry and then departed for the next stage of our journey.

As we scanned the map for the next place to visit, we decided on Porto. Getting slightly lost on the way, we eventually drove into the centre of Porto, a thriving city on the river. Tattered, weathered but majestically beautiful, it's the kind of place where I could picture poets smoking pipes as they mused on the finer things of life, drinking obligatory glasses of port.

The journey had not been straightforward. We had got lost several times and had accidentally skipped motorway tolls. When we had at last arrived, it was time to explore. Half the team went to do coffee, but the other half was set on checking out some of the city's busy streets and the classical architecture by the river. The team said a prayer and we split, having arranged to reconvene for some mission later in the day.

Jon and I had enjoyed wandering the streets, but when we arrived back at the vehicles, ready to feed the meter, there was no sign of the rest of the team. We waited, surprised that no one else from the team was about. Suddenly we heard shrieks as members of the team dashed towards us along the congested street, disappearing momentarily behind vehicles that separated us.

'They're here!' came the screams of Jo, Terri and Yamima. Broad smiles filled their faces as they strode towards us, brimming with enthusiasm. 'The Italians are here!' Excited laughter and a look of almost wonderment transcended as they chirped away merrily. 'God has given us another chance – a chance to pray with them.'

I have to say that I was taken aback by the whole thing. The continual prayers for the Italians had all seemed a bit over the top, but God had pretty miraculously hooked us up with them again. Grabbed by the arms, I was quickly whisked to the coffee shop where the rest of the team were sat among the four Italians. Everyone's face was beaming.

The coffee shop was situated on a busy street corner, with the continual sound of rumbling vehicles passing by. Everyone was perched outside under the shade of umbrellas. As I probed for the full story, it turned out that the Italians had spotted members of the team as they came round the corner. As the two groups were reunited, the Italians jovially exclaimed, 'Jesus has brought us back together!'

'Amen!' responded the team members in unison.

Alexandro had thick dark dreads and a stoned look about him. He was super cool with the situation and seemed pretty relaxed. He was meticulously rolling a cigarette as we began to talk. I asked him if we had freaked him out, but he just offered a subtle smile and said, 'You guys are cool,' before chuckling to himself. We talked about travelling, coffee and faith, and the conversation flowed naturally as different team members took their turn.

We sat around talking, ordering a second drink and then a third. We then invited them for food and within a few moments we were in a restaurant with hearty servings of meat served on skewers suspended in mid-air by individual table stands. The animated conversations continued and intensified. I looked down the table, watching the team answering questions and sharing testimony. As I got stuck into the food, I prayed that in our enthusiasm we would continue to hear the voice of Jesus.

As dialogue continued over coffee, Dave and I left to get the vehicles, which were overdue on the meter. We got back to discover that conversations had continued over yet another cup of coffee. Jo and Sarah were in deep discussion with Alexandro. Jo felt a prompting to ask him about a broken heart and from there the conversation moved on to Jesus the healer. In a concoction of languages that Sarah had the dubious task of translating, Alexandro admitted to having a broken heart and feelings of guilt in relation to an ex-girlfriend. Suddenly the conversation got very intense. Jo spoke and Alexandro listened and nodded, asked and queried.

The conversation ended in prayer. Jo prayed that Alexandro would know that his broken heart and his guilt could be sorted by Jesus, and only by Jesus. As Jo said 'Amen', Alexandro locked eyes with Jo and told Sarah in French, 'I understood. I have hope.'

It was with tear-filled eyes that goodbyes were said. This time the team had definitely prayed with each guy. They were not going to blow another opportunity. There had been no dramatic conversion to cap off the story, but as the van pulled away Alexandro waved to Jo, clenched his fist and tapped his heart as his eyes welled up with tears. He tapped his heart again, confirming that he had understood the truth of Jo's prayer.

As we searched for somewhere to camp, Jo wept. She brushed the tears from her eyes and murmured, 'They're so close. I could see it in Alexandro's eyes. He is so broken and needs Jesus.'

So once again we prayed for the Italians.

* * *

MOORS, *The Columbia Encyclopedia*, Sixth Edition, 2006.

Tim Dowley, *The History of Christianity*, Lion Publishing, 1990.

6

Hidden Treasure

We pulled up alongside an old boat in a dimly lit fishing community. The van was quiet and most of the team had dropped off to sleep. The air was hot and stuffy, and drowsiness was in abundance. The drive had been tough. We had no set destination to set up camp and so we had been trying to locate a deserted beach with a map of the entire continent of Europe. Definitely not ideal.

It was gone 1 am and I had been fighting to keep my eyes open as we desperately searched for an off-the-beaten-track-type location to sleep. This fishing community was definitely the back of beyond. It was an ideal place for a horror movie setting. An eerie silence was punctured only by the irritating buzz of an electric pylon.

I went for a quick recce of the area and came across a small stretch of beach. Further in the distance, I could make out that the beach enlarged into a more recognisable bay. My eyes strained to see more clearly in the haze of lights from nearby houses.

The air was salty and warm, and I jogged back to get the team and let them know that we had arrived at tonight's four-star accommodation. I suggested that we stay on the beach near the cars, but various members of the team preferred the bay because it looked more serene. So, with sleeping bags and pillows grasped in tired arms, we began making our way along the narrow beach to the bay that lay a few hundreds metres ahead. The pairs of footprints left their mark on the soft sand as we journeyed on.

It wasn't long before Becky screamed, 'There's something crawling on my feet!'

In a split moment we looked down to see hundreds of tiny crabs scurrying around on the sand beneath us. Becky's alerting scream was followed by an echo of other screams as the girls' sleepy demeanour disappeared and they began to run towards the lights of the nearby concrete road.

It took me the next 20 minutes to determine that the initial segment of beach by the vehicles had no crabs, spiders, worms or any other creepy crawlies on it. With a torch in one hand, I scanned the sand 'just to make sure' and the team finally agreed to sleep on the beach. Where else were we going to stay? With a comedy set of 'goodnights', just like on *The Waltons*, 13 sleeping bags huddled together for safety gradually became motionless as the sand was moulded around the gently sleeping bodies.

* * *

As the morning sun began to appear, the 13 sleeping bags still lay motionless on the beach. The occasional dog walker and scruffy fisherman wandered by, taking hardly any notice of the sleeping team.

With the lull of waves, I woke Jon and we headed off in

pursuit of an early morning surf. The last few days had been quite intense and it was great to get away from the group for a little while. We recounted the story of the screaming girls the night before as we drove down the coast checking various beaches for waves big enough to surf.

The 'I'm going for a surf' line allowed me to be free from the whole group for a little while; to get perspective on the mission and to listen to what God was saying. Jon and I chatted about whether we were on mission or holiday and we both agreed that it had definitely been mission. Living together in such a confined space was making the Road Trip begin to feel like an episode of *Big Brother*. It was good to get a breather. We talked and prayed, and continued to scan the coast for waves.

With no decent waves in sight, we went for coffee and crois-sants before napping in the car while we waited for the VW van to join us with the rest of the team. It would have to be the morn-ing that we snuck off that the VW got a flat tyre. Amazingly this had happened just outside a car mechanic's, and with eight pretty girls on board they had managed to get the mechanic to change the tyre for free. Another opportunity to share the gospel opened up and with a gift of cold beers and a couple of tracts, God was at work.

* * *

There are some days when you stumble across things that you just do not expect. When you are journeying with friends in unknown lands, that sense of adventure drives you in pursuit of discovery. I am the sort of guy who likes to drive until something looks interesting and then stop to investigate. When on Road Trip, this urge within only increased. The excitement of pulling over to explore, and occasionally finding jewels off the beaten track, is exhilarating.

Bom Jesus was such a jewel. It was the sign to Bom Jesus that had caught our eye, and although we initially turned up at a psychiatric hospital, we eventually found a lay-by with a sign for the cathedral.

Not expecting to find much, I jumped out of the van, darted over the fence and snuck round the trees to see if this was a place worthy of a break. The moment I turned the corner, there was a sudden visual explosion as my eyes were bombarded with the most amazing staircase that erupted into the cathedral above. With green trees to either side, the hundreds of perfectly aligned steps were an unexpected marvel full of history. Framed with the blue sky above, this was most definitely a Kodak moment.

Back at the van I exclaimed, 'You've gotta see this – it's awesome.' As the rest of the team assembled in the lay-by, I made them close their eyes so that I could escort them to the viewpoint at the bottom of the staircase. Once positioned, they opened their eyes to suddenly get the full impact of the staircase before them.

'Wow, man, this is mental,' said Dave as a series of gasps escaped from their stunned faces. The grey staircase, with its whitewashed walls, snaked through a series of statues and fountains. Each statue told a story. They were carved from rock and depicted biblical heroes of faith, with segments of Scripture etched in the wall beside them.

Like children in a Toys R Us megastore, we splintered off in a world of discovery, reading the pieces of Scripture, photographing the various statues or playing in the fountains. We excitedly ascended the mighty staircase with the occasional prayer pit-stop that distracted our attention from the climb – momentary pauses for reflection on the balconies between the layers of stairs.

The staircase construction had started in 1722 and it was amazing to think of the tens of thousands of pilgrims who had reached this place and let out the same gasps as we had done moments earlier. We discovered that pilgrims traditionally climbed the stairs on their knees in penance. With hundreds of steps, I was glad that I believed in the abundant grace of Jesus and that my theology had no need for penance.

As I pictured the many people who had climbed these steps on their knees, I was challenged by the fact that perhaps we sometimes take the grace of Jesus too easily. As I was driving over the course of the Road Trip, people had taken it in turns to read Bonhoeffer to me to keep me awake. Jo was a big fan and had often opted to sit in the passenger seat as we discussed our practical response to his thinking. The idea of cheap grace kept coming up in his writing: the idea that we quickly forget the cost Christ paid for our sins and that we frequently fail to live a life of real repentance.

As I took a moment to pray, I washed my hands in the fountains that splashed into pools of water on each landing. The cleansing water that wiped away the sweat and the grime filtered through the very centre of the staircase, bubbling away as a profound symbol of the Spirit of God being in this place.

We gradually assembled at the top of the stairs, sharing some of the things that we felt God had been saying to us. Many of the group had been dubious about visiting Catholic places and God being 'present'. It stemmed from our very judgemental, evangelical–charismatic upbringing, which implicitly taught us that Catholicism is just 'religious' rather than being about a relationship with God. But as God had spoken to us in this Catholic cathedral, it reminded me of the verse from Genesis: 'Surely God was in this place and we didn't even realise it' (Genesis 28:16).

I still have great problems with some of the Roman Catholic doctrine, but I am sure that when I get to glory God will not say, 'Well done, Andy. You had the perfect theology.' I am sure that there are major shortfalls in some of the things I believe, and I am just glad that a God we could fully understand wouldn't be a God big enough to meet all of our needs. There remains that mystery element.

The cathedral took pride of place at the top of the staircase and after we had convened we set to exploring the main sanctuary. The cathedral was busy, with tourists swarming around the entrance. They had shuffled off coaches on quick tours of numerous sites. As coaches arrived and then quickly departed, they had missed out on the delights of the staircase below. So often we rush through life, focused upon the destination rather than enjoying the journey.

* * *

I entered the gigantic cathedral and it offered pleasant shade and coolness after the beating sun outside. A musty smell with a touch of incense filled the wide dark space. The front of the vestry depicted a life-size model of the crucifixion. The infamous Good Friday scene and the dim lighting painted a powerful picture. A picture that required a reaction. The ornate and elaborate depiction of the cross was very unfamiliar. It was very different from the bland white walls of most of the churches I visit.

In the side chapel, the walls were covered with letters and photographs and even crutches, testifying to miraculous healings that had taken place. Photos of the sick before and after were powerful suggestions that these miracles were not some figment of the imagination. As the team studied different letters and testimonies, a montage of questions was raised about healing, faith and God. We all knew of miracles, but we also all knew of those who were living in sickness. It was at this point that we gathered on a nearby bandstand and began to sing songs of worship to our God – our God who was so beyond our under-standing, yet so personal, that He had chosen to come and be with us.

As we continued to sing, coaches carried on pulling up and pulling away, and people watched us express our faith in song. We stopped singing to pray, while Jon continued to strum in the background. Jo, resting her Bible on the side of the stand, began to share: 'If this is a place of miracles, then we need to ask God that we might see more of His power. More of His power at work on this trip . . . in our lives . . . and in Portugal.'

She fumbled through the tatty weathered pages of the New Testament to read from James: 'The prayer of a righteous man is powerful and effective . . .' (5:16). She went on to share about Elijah's prayer for rain and then challenged us that we might pray for rain for Portugal. Portugal was in the middle of a serious drought, and bush fires had kicked off all around the country. They desperately needed rain, and as Elijah had prayed for rain with faith, Jo lay down the challenge that we too might pray in faith for rain in Portugal. As we began to lift our arms up in prayer and catapult prayers of faith into the arms of God, a group of tourists began to watch intently – confused by our irregular antics. We continued without caring much of what others thought. I wonder if we would have had the same boldness if we had been in Stockport? Our prayers came to a close and our descent back down the steps to the vehicles began.

We never saw rain throughout the trip. It would have been a great story if the heavens had opened and it had started pelting down the moment we said 'Amen'! But it didn't. I don't know why, but it didn't. Just like healings, sometimes God does the incredible, but sometimes He chooses not to. But I guess, once again, who understands God fully? We all need to keep this childlike faith.

* * *

When it comes to buying surfboards, I have some idea of what I am looking for, but rosaries are a different matter. I entered the Bom Jesus gift shop before getting back into the car and I knew that I only had a few minutes to make a purchase. I thought it would be a simple task, buying a rosary. I had wanted one for a while, but I hadn't come across many 'rosary selling' shops in south-west London. Now I was in Bom Jesus and this seemed to be a significant place; the kind of place that demands a memento. A rosary would be perfect.

My eyes were overwhelmed at the sight of the cabinet that was overflowing with rosaries. There was an assortment of colours, a range of sizes and a multitude of price tags. I took a couple of them off the shelf to get a feel for them – the same way people feel carpets with their hands in a carpet store. I hadn't got a clue what I was looking for, so I just stared at the cabinet glumly.

Finally, I chose one. Running the string through my fingers, I counted the beads off quickly, one at a time. With a quick check of the price tag, I handed it over to the cashier and my purchase was complete. Five euros well spent.

I think rosaries are cool. Maybe that's just because they are foreign to my church background. It's funny how things from differing church traditions can sometimes be trendy just because they're different. Maybe I also think rosaries are cool because they have the potential to be a little controversial. I can imagine the look on some of my more conservative friends' faces if I were to pull the rosary out at a prayer meeting. Would they think that I had lost the plot and was now worshipping Mary?

But I hadn't just bought the rosary to stand out; neither had I bought it to have the latest Christian fashion accessory or to be a bit controversial. I had bought the rosary to help myself pray, because, well, to be honest, I often find prayer difficult. I try to be in conversation with God throughout the day, listening to Him and sharing my day with Him. This seems quite natural. But when it comes to hour-long sessions of sustained intercession, I find it tough. My mind wanders and I end up on some random line of thought, like how many films I can name starring Catherine Zeta-Jones.

Throughout church history, it has been movements of prayer that have underpinned moves of God. I want to be better at the whole prayer thing because I want my desperation for another move of God to be illustrated in my prayer life. Creative ways to pray help me stay focused on Jesus, whether that be prayer wrestling, prophetic painting or, nowadays, carrying a rosary.

The rosary I bought had 50 beads, neatly grouped in 'decades' of ten. It felt very new. I later researched rosaries to discover that my new purchase would not have been recognised by the original users. It was around the year 800 when the use of the rosary was first introduced. The Irish monks would daily recite 150 psalms as part of their prayerful existence. People living in the surrounding villages wanted to join in the prayer activity, but they could not read and learning the psalms by heart was no easy task. Instead, they began to respond to each psalm with the

Lord's Prayer. In time, they began carrying pouches with 150 stones, so that they could maintain this practice of praying 150 times, even when they were out in the fields. The pouch with 150 stones was soon replaced by a string with 150 knots. Much lighter!

Over the centuries, the rosary was adapted into a piece of string with 50 beads, which was to be prayed through three times a day. In many Roman Catholic churches today, the rosary is used to contemplate the face of Jesus through the eyes of His mother Mary. The Mysteries, which are episodes from Christ's life, form a framework for this meditation.

I looked down at my hand as I strode back to the car, watching as the light-brown beads slid between my fingers. I planned to use the rosary for different things as the weeks passed by: for praying for 50 people who did not know Christ, or as a means to thank God for 50 things, or maybe to confess 50 things that I had done wrong. The light brown of the beads wrapped around my fingers contrasted with the tanned backs of my hands. They somehow looked more distinguished nursing a rosary. The small cross at the end of the beads swung with the motion of each step, reminding me of the centrality of the cross in prayer.

As I left the staircase behind for other pilgrims to stumble across, the team jumped back into the vehicles and headed off in search of further treasure. Another place had been explored. Another tradition had been unravelled. Another opportunity had been seized. Another day road tripping with God.

* * *

The Lonely Planet Guide to Portugal, Lonely Planet Publications, 2004.

Mike McCormack, *The Origin of the Rosary*, www.aoh.com/history/archive/rosary.htm

7

Proper Pilgrims

The journey so far had brought us into a variety of rare experiences and into communion with, well, rare people. There had been moments of ecstasy as we had been reunited with the Italians, worshipped God and prayed on the edge of the world at St Vincent. There had been moments of frustration with lost keys, bad directions and karaoke bars. And then there had been moments where God had begun to speak. Where God had begun to break some of our hearts for the lost, for the poor, for a bigger perspective of Europe. We were being transformed.

When you journey with strangers, you quickly become intimate, sharing life's experiences together. As the late afternoon sun began its descent, and having inadvertently driven up one-way streets the wrong way, I looked back over my shoulder to see my fellow pilgrims deep in conversation.

The initial conversations that mark the beginning of a trip – the 'What do you do?' type questions, with their pre-fixed, perfectly crafted responses – had quickly begun to recede. Over the course of just a few days, people had begun to lower their masks and talk about who they were rather than just what they did. We were becoming a living community.

The quality of conversation began to reach a whole new plain. Past the niceties there comes a point when nothing is 'off limits'. Open dialogue with rare honesty begins to approach life's difficult questions, temptations and past hurts. This is what church community should really be about and we were living it.

Jon, with his eyes firmly fixed on the road ahead and his hands casually resting on the steering wheel, began to share how God was teaching him the basics of his faith all over again. After years of being a Christian, he was rediscovering that God loved him.

He shared his experience in Peru, where he had been leading a mission team with YWAM. He hadn't overly enjoyed leading the team. He had struggled to keep the whole team on board with the plans and he had struggled to keep them all happy. This is never easy and I could empathise with his experience!

A key part of that mission had been to set up a surf contest. While balancing team dynamics, he had taken on lots of the organisational work, which had included printing fliers and posters, getting permission to use the beach, setting up stands on the shore and sourcing prizes for the competition winners. Organising the whole event had been one huge battle. But with everything in order, he was expecting great things.

But there was one big problem. On the day of the competition, no one turned up. Not a single surfer. He shared how devastated he had been, while putting on a brave face for his team. As a result he had got really angry with God. With the sole motive of setting up a surf competition so that others might come to know Jesus, God had let him down. In a word, he was 'gutted'.

As he told the story, he occasionally looked in the rear-view mirror to check that he had everyone's attention, and he had. We quietly hung on to his every word as his story unfolded and his raw emotions were emerging.

But as he had got angry with God, God had challenged him. He felt that God had said, 'Will you only serve Me if you have a fruitful ministry? It's easy to serve Me when you have a success-ful ministry, but will you do it just because you love Me, and because I love you?' Jon had been on a journey of rediscovering God's love and serving just for the joy of serving.

His words challenged us all and as we began to share stories of what God was teaching us, there were moments when we would pause for prayer. Conversations that are seasoned with prayer are important conversations. Snippets of life story were woven together with biblical truths that might never be shared publicly again. Each story, profound in its honesty, opened my understanding to another aspect of the character of God.

Terri was next to share. She liked to laugh and had a mischie-vous side that sometimes involved mooning. Her speech was flavoured with the occasional swear word, which was quickly fol-lowed by 'Oh, I'm so sorry'. I loved that realness about her. She had only been a Christian a couple of years and, at the age of 18, she was never afraid of asking those difficult questions that Christians often sweep under the carpet. She had been nervous about coming on the trip initially. She questioned whether she knew enough about God to go on mission. She also feared mak-ing a fool of herself with her lack of biblical knowledge. But as she openly shared her journey, it was clear that she was hungry to understand more of who God is. Best of all she was willing to be changed.

She combed her ginger hair back with the palm of her hand as she spoke. 'My faith has been real gradual,' she explained. 'There has been no bright light, but when I joined the local church youth group, I met people who cared for me – people who just kinda loved me.' She wanted what they had – not all of the stuffiness of the church services, but the reality of this love.

As she spoke she often paused, biting her lip as she waited for the next words to come. She had given her life to God, but she still had questions. She found her whole relationship with God much harder than she had envisioned. She found it harder than relationships with physical people she could have a coffee with.

'It is so hard trusting God and it's so hard just reading the Bible and spending time praying,' she said. *For sure*, I remember thinking, *prayer and Bible reading are difficult disciplines*.

Her biggest issue was knowing whether the Bible was definitely all true and as she shared, different members of the team started to offer set answers – the kind you are taught in Sunday school. But I don't think Terri wanted pappy answers. She just wanted us to know where she was coming from. Her journey with God was not a journey with all the answers, but it was a journey with a set starting point, and that point was Jesus. Her relationship with God was not going to be easy, but she was persevering. She had found something of God and she wasn't going to let go; or was it that God was not going to let go of her?

Terri's sharing gave me a further insight into life with God – this journey that provokes new questions. I find it so difficult when often in Christian circles people claim to have a boring testimony, for when God is at work, life can never be boring. The Creator of the mountains and the oceans is at work intimately in our lives. It always staggers me.

After a while, there was silence as people were left to their own thoughts, their eyes flickering as they looked out of the wide windows, a flume of roadside green cascading by. As I turned to look out of the front window, and Jon continued to drive on, God confirmed once again that this was not just a mission. Road Trip was also a pilgrimage. We were journeying as friends and journeying with God. Each day there were new opportunities and possibilities. This is how life should always be. At every fork in the road, new adventures lie ahead.

* * *

This fork had led us deep into Spain, and as we approached Santiago de Compostela I was excited about visiting this new city. It was set before us awaiting exploration. It was a place of real heritage. A gigantic cathedral stood in prime position at the very centre of the city, surrounded by a tightly packed old town with narrow streets and traditional craft shops. As we drove into the city, it felt as though we were entering a film set for *The Canterbury Tales*.

I had read *The Canterbury Tales* as a set text during my GCSEs and had been intrigued by the tales that were told as people embarked on such a pilgrimage. People had journeyed for many reasons. Countless knights had journeyed to Santiago on horseback to receive God's blessing before galloping off to distant lands for battle. Some had travelled with an economic objective, selling their wares to pilgrims along the way. Others had journeyed to escape punishment for law-breaking. Others were genuine pilgrims in pursuit of penance or a greater encounter with God. They had travelled by foot or on horseback, taking refuge in the monasteries and churches along the way. Their journeys had often taken months as they travelled from far-flung places.

People continue to take this challenge today along the same old routes. Each year people travel hundreds of miles by foot to reach Santiago. Each pilgrim travels with a different modern-day objective. Some get sponsored as they take the challenge to raise money for charity; others make the pilgrimage as part of their personalised fitness regime; and others make the journey for true spiritual enlightenment.

But I felt as if we had cheated. We had entered Santiago in vehicles. We had driven at speed and enjoyed considerably more comfort than other pilgrims. It was like crossing the finishing line of a marathon without actually running the race. We had no blisters.

And we stood out as different too. Unlike the authentic pilgrims, who could be identified by their staff in hand and a cockle shell fastened to their cloak, we were wearing our bright red Road Trip Mission t-shirts. The symbol of the cockle shell stems back to a story of a Portuguese knight who fell into the sea, along with his frightened horse. Legend has it that the knight was rescued and his clothing was covered in cockle shells. Ever since, people have worn them as a symbol of God's protection.

Santiago seems to be a place of truth and fiction, faith and fantasy. It has been birthed in legend. The old pilgrimage route that leads to Santiago is called the Way of St James, and it has been attracting pilgrims since the ninth century. St James, the brother of John and one of the twelve disciples, supposedly brought the gospel to Spain. In about AD 810, Bishop Theodomir claimed to have found James's body and this discovery helped inspire the Christians in their bloody battles against the Muslim Moors. Legend has it that St James himself, who had been dead for centuries, routed the enemy with a white standard painted with a red cross.

As dusk settled, like a blurred line between night and day, I wasn't quite sure where truth ended and fiction began. The messy stories of tradition clouded my mind. It is no wonder that some people doubt the claims of the church when so much legend has been piled onto the gospel over the centuries. As people like Terri grapple with the validity of the Bible, it is important for the focus to be on Jesus rather than on dead saints fighting battles, and knights covered with cockle shells.

As I grappled with these stories, I was searching for truth. In a world polluted with deception, being a Christian is about being on a journey in the search for truth; in the search for greater intimacy with Jesus. The pilgrimage is life.

* * *

After a long day of travelling, we tucked into a pretty shocking meal of pigs' ears. I guess that you have to try these things when travelling, but pigs' ears were a big mistake and they left that rather unpleasant aftertaste that sinks to the back of your throat and reappears at intervals throughout the following week.

Pigs' ears were followed by the much more endearing thought of a bed. After nights of sleeping rough and the endless miles that I had clocked up, it was like stepping out of an adventure for a moment to enjoy the finer things of life. The open window allowed a gentle breeze to move through the room and I disappeared off into a deep, deep sleep – the kind you read about in children's nursery rhymes.

So it all started the next morning as I imagined answering the phone in my dream, except that I actually had the phone in my hand and could hear Ellie rapidly speaking in a very concerned Yorkshire accent. 'Andy – get up! They're about to tow the car away.'

I sprang out of bed as I tried to work out where I was and my sleepy eyes caught sight of the light that was streaking through the curtain, almost blinding me. With one hand on the phone I barked instructions for Ellie to stop the car from being towed away at all costs, even if it meant lying in front of the tow truck. The other hand scrambled to find shorts and loop them over my feet and then grabbed a t-shirt. I then made a bee-line for the door before striding back to grab the car keys off the desk.

Down in the courtyard, I looked like a washed-up shipwreck survivor with bad bed hair and no sandals. As awake as a dinosaur, I hurried over to the car, which was sitting on the back of a tow truck, while Sarah and Lisa tried to persuade the parking attendant to give us our car back. As the scene began to unravel like a comedy sitcom sequence, Chris arrived, having followed me down, clutching his video camera to capture the mayhem.

We managed to get the car back, but at a price, and the van had also been ticketed. Though we haggled the cost down, we still had to pay a ridiculous ransom. Apparently certain markings on the floor mean no parking from 7 am till 3 pm, but what chance had we to know? With the words of God's love resonating from the conversations the day before, I thought I would at least give the traffic warden an opportunity to receive Christ, so I shared about the ransom Jesus had paid. A bemused look crossed his face as we swapped the receipt for the car charge with the bright red tract. And best of all, Chris had it all on camera.

This eventful start to the morning was followed by a strong espresso as the team converged on the small coffee shop beneath the hostel. With bags stowed away, we headed for the cathedral to grab a good look at this pilgrim destination.

* * *

The square was engulfed in noise as tourists bustled around in packs, following tour guides as if they were magnets. Each guide spoke in a different language, spewing out rehearsed monologues of factual information as sightseers leaned inward to feed their minds with knowledge. Queues of tourists swayed, while people pushed their way towards entrances and streams of people fought their way to exit. One grand movement of people pushing in different directions. The large cathedral stood out like a proud and obnoxious monument that required attention, dominating the local topography.

It was a bizarre scene to watch as tourists mobbed this place of apparent worship. The square was a cocktail of sound. The crowds snapped pictures as they congregated in the square. The cockle-wearing pilgrims exiting the cathedral alongside us looked lost in the sea of tourists who were more concerned with photos than worship.

We dispersed into the cathedral to see the sights and emerged voicing our disappointment. The architecture was pretty cool, but the entire interior focused around a statue of St James, not Jesus. 'It symbolises how man always wants to be in the most important place,' shared Jo. I thought that was very profound. By 'man' I presume she meant 'men and women'.

Mankind wanting to take the place of God; pride, the origin of sin? Bom Jesus had been all about Jesus, but Santiago seemed to be all about James. A great man I'm sure, but he wasn't the Son of God.

Santiago, in my opinion, was not quite the destination I had hoped for. It definitely wasn't worth the parking fines! There had been no great epiphany. Though the destination had been a disappointment, the journey had been momentous. In our world, focused on achievement and arriving, perhaps we too often focus our faith upon the destination rather than enjoying the journey.

Over the years I have led many young people to Jesus. It is a real privilege to be involved in someone's story at the moment when they accept His forgiveness; at the moment when they replace themselves at the centre of the cathedral of their lives with Jesus. I remember that in my early 20s I used to think that that was it; job done. They had met with God and were on track to destination heaven. I still believe that, but now I concentrate on more than the final destination.

I was discovering that the journey only begins with that intro-duction to Jesus. I am continually on a pilgrimage with God, and I will never get to that point on earth when I have made it as a Christian. I am set for eternity, but I am still journeying. I am still being changed, and that for me is what pilgrimage is all about. There is still so much more of God that waits to be discovered. There is still so much truth to be revealed.

We are all on a pilgrimage. Once we accept Jesus, the destina-tion is heaven, but it's not just about the destination; it's also about the journey. The journey is life.

* * *

Ada Alvey, *In Search of St James: Cornwall to Compostela*, Dyllansow Truran, 1989.

Larry D. Benson, *The Riverside Chaucer*, Oxford University Press, 1988.

8

Christian Night

As I carved into the face of the wave, cutting shapes in the perfect glass-like conditions, there was an overwhelming surge of energy that ricocheted right through me – a tingly sensation. The kind of feeling you get when you are taking a risk but enjoying the thrill. I felt so alive as I looked down the wall of water that was lined up ahead of me, enticing me to plan my route of turns. The ten-foot face of the wave had plenty of power and I stalled the board momentarily before charging along the line. Words can't describe the utter thrill I felt as I raced down the collapsing wave and fellow surfers hollered.

The surf session ended rather unfortunately though. Not because of injury or near drowning, but because of our location. As I began to make my way towards the beach, lying flat on my board and being carried rapidly by the white water, I looked up to see a rather horrific sight: completely naked OAP holiday-makers. Weaving between naked French men and women, I dared not close my eyes for fear of bouncing right into them. Instead, my innocence was ruined. Old naked people clutching beach balls and working on their all-over tans almost put me off surfing for life. I made a mental check not to drift into naturist areas again. I guess this was my welcome to the real France.

* * *

We had actually arrived in France a couple of days earlier, just in time for one of the biggest surf comps in Europe, with competitors from around the world. As I pulled the VW Transporter up to the beach, the sound of perfect waves breaking in the background squeezed through the window as I gradually rolled it down. The sounds coming from within the vehicle were slightly less soothing. We had voted on the all-night drive to avoid the dense summertime holiday traffic that is notorious for miles of tailbacks. We had also wanted to skim some money off the budget. But the drive had taken its toll on the team and tired eyes readjusted to the light as the sun rose over the sandy car park.

Within moments, charismatic Rich had bounced up to the car like an excited dog bounding up to a newcomer at the door. A manly embrace followed as I was introduced to the guys who had already trekked down to France with him. Simon was a South African, or Saffa as they are affectionately known. He had come to teach some of the Road Trippers the art of surfing. Not yet a Christian, Simon was a qualified instructor who had travelled the world in search of perfect waves. He was a photographer and cameraman, hoping to get some quality footage of the comp that lay ahead.

As the team began to stumble out of the vehicles and into the fresh morning air, tension started to build. We could not get into the beachside accommodation for several hours. Bleary eyes were clearly not impressed and the idea of sitting in a car park for half a day was not greeted with much enthusiasm. I, on the other hand, was stoked to be in France, and the appeal of the waves meant that I was quite happy to surf before sleeping.

As the reality of the car park wait hit, surfers began to stream past, being lulled ever closer by the majestic sound of crashing waves. Within moments, my board was beneath my arm and I was almost skipping towards the water's edge to get in my first session in the tepid waters of France.

* * *

Later that day, the team rested as I manoeuvred my way down the toll roads and into Biarritz airport to pick up the rest of the team coming for the French leg of the trip. I greeted the weary travellers with cold Cokes, and we then began the 25-minute drive back to the accommodation, which was now ready for occupation. The vehicles were brimming with chatter as people adjusted to the bright summer's sun.

On top of the British contingent, there were a couple of international friends to be collected that afternoon. I had first met these guys in the Alps as we had missioned it together in the snowboard resort of Les Deux Alpes. Oliver was from Austria, a successful businessman with broad shoulders and a muscular physique. Mirijam was from Switzerland and oozed cool as she beamed with smiles.

The French coastline is littered with quaint seaside towns and the occasional Catholic church steeple punctuating the horizon. I fought back the tiredness as we glided along the open coastal road, air bursting through the open windows.

With the team in place, the week commenced with an overview from Rich and me. We introduced the French pastor and his family who were to be our partners for the week. They were a new set of comrades to work alongside and they were ready to follow up any locals who responded during the mission week.

Bernard was a tall man, with hair that abounded from his ears and neck. He spoke good English with a strong French accent and gestured with his hands as he shared. He had started a small fellowship with his family a few miles from the beach. Their church vestry was part of their home and they lived in a simple house. Bernard had seven children; his family was almost a church in itself!

Bernard had toiled tirelessly for the kingdom and had seen slow but steady growth. He was completely isolated from other evangelical churches and although he was slightly more tradi-tional than Rich and I, he was so excited to have people sharing in his mission and assisting his local church that he put all differ-ences aside and welcomed us in. In the UK, when we look to partner with local churches to host short-term mission teams, we sometimes have to twist a pastor's arm to get them on board. It was so refreshing to have a local church so thankful to have us before we had even done anything!

Bernard shared with the group, 'I am delighted to have you here with us. Thank you for coming and sharing Jesus. We need your help in France.' He explained something of the area's cul-tural context and the secular worldview. France was not an easy place to be a Christian and many evangelical churches were seen by the state as being cults. Street preaching had now been made illegal. Yet despite all this opposition, Bernard had a passion for the lost and was clinging on to the promises of God.

The team had soaked in the introductory session. They dis-persed around the campsite green in huddles of prayer. Rich had dictated a list of prayer requests, tilting his head as though his memory was drip-feeding a list of things to his mouth. One of the key things to pray for was the end of week event.

The final event was to be the pinnacle of the week. It was entitled The Sundowner and was to be hosted in the Crème Café, which sat just yards from the competition beach in the car park, slightly hidden by towering sand dunes. The main bar area extended onto wooden decking overlooking a massive car park. This was where I had seen the Christian Surfers' outreach event almost a year ago. It was like returning to a sacred space where I had seen God at work before.

Rich had arrived some days earlier with his car overloaded with mission resources, including French surfer Bibles, decks, football goal posts and an assortment of tracts. He had stacked his Volvo to capacity and it had crawled down the coast at only 50 mph.

As prayers came to a close, the plans were hatched. The team had tripled in size and now had a more international flavour and a broader spectrum of ages. Our youngest team member was now Daniella, who was a bold and confident twelve-year-old. She was all set for her first overseas mission.

The team had to be divided and the whole mission needed a tighter format to make sure that the week would run smoothly. Saffa Simon would co-ordinate morning surf lessons, while the afternoon was a cocktail of beach footy, bottled water giveaways and flyering. With a mixture of evening worship, public Bible studies and detached work in the evenings, the programme was created. The team was ready for action.

* * *

The French coast is infamous for its great waves; beach break barrels to be precise. However, the miles of open beach mean that it is easily susceptible to the local wind, which can destroy the clean lines of swell that surfers dream of. But the forecast for the week was exceptional, with a massive swell and little wind.

The Quicksilver Pro is one of the biggest surf contests in Europe. Its location marks out some of the best sandbanks along the coast. The comp is like an oasis of colour along the stretch of yellow that disappears into the distance. Huge flags with a variety of surf brands adorn the framework of the portable cabins and tents. The whole area is branded with a concoction of logos fighting for space, ranging from beer brands to mobile phone companies.

In the early morning the comp seems like a ghost town except for the occasional surfer paddling out for a dawn session, but by mid-morning, the site is infiltrated with tanned surfers and ladies in bikinis. A barrage of languages trickles through the crowd and a selection of national flags litters the beach. It was here that much of our day-to-day mission would take place.

Each afternoon the team spilled out of our resort with football goal posts and tracts, coated in Factor 50 and filled with a sense of adventure. Topped up on a cracking French lunch and fuelled on a quick prayer session, conversations were sparked, and people were prayed for.

I took on more of an overseeing role, co-ordinating resources and checking everyone was OK. Stumbling across the team running international football games with their finely erected set of goal posts (all the way from Weston-super-Mare), I joined in as the UK took on France. Games were followed by conversations, as water was chugged down gasping mouths. With broken French, I introduced myself as a *cretin* (which means knucklehead – well, that is the polite translation) rather than a *chrétien* (Christian). A classic schoolboy error, I think you'll agree.

Yet with the help of Sarah, who had grown up in France, a short conversation about Zidane had preambled into what I did for a living. Within a few short sentences, I was trying to pray over the young French man's ankle as we asked God to heal the injury that had plagued him for years.

Whenever I pray for the sick, there is always a twinge of nerves as I lie in wait wondering if God's healing will be made manifest. I always pray with my eyes open, just in case I see the entire leg, or whatever I am praying for, morph into a new shape. I would hate to miss it with my eyes tightly scrunched closed.

As I prayed, my eyes switched their focus from his ankle to his eyes and I watched him relax into what was happening. There was no miraculous spark, but with a polite 'thank you' he explained that it now felt a bit better. With an exchange of smiles, we went our separate ways.

* * *

It was time for Rich and me to plan the end of week event. We were soon at the Crème Café, sipping Cokes and conversing with Max. Max was the bar manager and he was a very business-minded guy aged 30-something. He had short dark hair and loved the summer months, hanging out with guys who moved to this corner of France for the season. He had been working here for a few years and he always wore thick black shades and a cheeky grin. He also loved to party and was always offering us a cold beer, no matter what the time of day.

'Last year was off the hook,' he exclaimed as he reminisced about the Christian Surfers' event. 'We love Christian night!' The previous year had been so successful and Max was keen for a repeat performance. It had been the biggest night of the year, with barrels of beer sold.

Deals were struck and we finished our Cokes, leaving the ice cubes rattling around the empty glass. We had opted to call the end of week party The Sundowner, to subtly dumb down the fact that this was a Jesus event. We had printed thousands of fliers to distribute to such an end. Max had a very different approach. He had produced posters and planted them around town, calling the event 'Christian Night'.

'Christian Night?' Rich and I both almost choked with a sense of 'He's got to be joking?'.

With a concerned look, Rich said, 'Err, are you sure that's the best title?'

Max nodded his head with utter confidence. 'Last year was so awesome . . . everyone has been waiting for another Christian Night – it's the best night of the year!' He seemed absolutely positive that calling the event 'Christian Night' would evoke a mass crowd. Who were we to argue?

As the week progressed, I remained dubious about 'Christian Night'. For one thing, in the UK the title would never work. It needed to be catchy and cool, and 'Christian Night' would have sent out completely the wrong message. We were also somewhat troubled to discover that our big finale party was going to clash with the Rip Curl party, which had a line-up of hot local talent and a wet t-shirt competition. Our event had the potential to go completely pear-shaped.

While the fliers were filtering their way along the expanse of beach, the event itself needed more work. We needed a band, a DJ, a projector screen. . . oh and a surf celebrity would really top it off! In fact the only thing we did have was a venue and a projector. The team were summoned to pray.

It felt like an episode of *Faking It* as we relayed to Jon the need to create a decent sounding band in just six days. With a selection of team members, he got to work, struggling to find songs that they all knew. A set of Delirious? songs would have to suffice, with the occasional Elton John track thrown in for good measure.

The DJ was also an issue. Dave had returned to the UK for a wedding and my turntable skills were somewhat lacking. I'm OK to DJ for a local youth group, but mixing at a beer-fuelled beach party is another issue. I turned on my mobile and scrolled through for any DJs who could be called upon with just six days' notice. The DJ Indian Rubberman, aka Paul Chowdry, was the man for the job, and after a little persuading he agreed to fly out with the quality airline Ryanair for a one-night mix.

The video screen was the other dilemma, but Rich seemed to have it under control. A chance meeting with the Quiksilver tour bus owner enabled him to blag the bus as a projector screen for the Christian Surfer movies that would be beamed onto its side.

Rich is one of those larger-than-life-type guys who have the ability to blag anything. He walks round with an air of confidence, verging on being cocky. This, combined with his natural charm, makes it hard to say 'no' to him. Not only had he blagged the Quiksilver bus, but he had also managed to get backstage passes at the surf comp, so that we could spend time witnessing to the pro surfers.

Our last challenge was to book a celebrity surfer and it was while we were at a guest-list post-competition party (that Rich had got us into) that our opportunity arose. Tom Curren, arguably one of the ten best surfers in the world and widely respected throughout surfing-dom, was sat at a table eating with his family. He was a committed Christian and had moved to France, having retired from the world circuit.

For the first time ever Rich seemed super nervous. Tom Curren was his boyhood hero and he had spent years sat in front of Curren's surf videos. This was his dream chance to see his childhood hero. It was like living in a *Jim'll Fix It* time warp as he cautiously walked over to Curren to ask if he would be our 'celebrity'. He already knew about Christian Night and had planned to come along with his guitar to play some music.

I like well-run events and am often embarrassed by shoddy church outreach events that are poorly put together. I had feared that Christian Night might well have taken that route, but God had worked – dare I say it? – miraculously. Everything seemed to be in place. To top it all off, Rip Curl had heard about Christian Night and had cancelled their party, fearful of the competition. Perhaps 'Christian Night' was a good name after all!

Meanwhile, Max had ordered his staff to chef up chilli for 500 people, perhaps with more faith than Rich and I had put together.

* * *

The Sunday morning service at Bernard's church had gone really well as I had shared, through Sarah the interpreter, the revolutionary nature of the gospel. After the service, the chairs had been pushed to one side and the team had gathered around the small congregation to pray for their continued day-in, day-out mission in the locality. Living in such a minority must seem overwhelming, and as we left, some of them promised to join us that evening at Christian Night. They were thankful for our encouragement and our very presence had helped rekindle some of their enthusiasm.

The big night finally arrived. After an abundance of prayer, there I was balanced precariously with one leg on the roof of our dirty white VW Transporter and my other knee squashed against the side of the Quicksilver tour bus, clutching a tablecloth and some Sellotape. I looked down to see Bernard and some of the church members below offering to assist. It was a privilege to be sharing in their mission field.

People had already started to arrive as I tried to rapidly cover the Quicksilver bus with tablecloths in order to create a big makeshift screen. Becky and a group of others were at the far end of the car park putting their finishing touches to a prayer tent they had created with tealights, sarongs, cushions, pens and paper. Their plan was to offer prayer to unsuspecting surfers as their quizzical looks drew them like a moth to a lightbulb.

As numbers grew and the bar veranda filled and then spilled out into the car park, the DJ Indian Rubberman got scratching. A chilled vibe engulfed the venue as the continual murmur of chatter floated into the sky and the sun began to set with flashes of red and orange.

Hannah and Terri had both stepped in to help serve the copious amounts of chilli and drinks to the swelling number of surfers. Jon's makeshift band kicked in and the acoustic sounds caused nearby conversations to conclude as feet tapped and heads nodded.

With top surf footage beamed onto the Quiksilver bus, it provided a wallpaper of light in the darkness as the sun disappeared behind its watery curtain. The team was at work, interspersed among the hundreds of surfers. This was how mission should be: lots of parties and lots of conversation.

With a week's hive of activity coming to a climax, it was time for a short gospel talk to capitalise on the conversations that were already being had. Rich was lined up to do it, but the stress of the evening was taking its toll. He was the only one who knew how the PA worked and he turned to me, asking, 'Andy, you have something you can share. Can you share the gospel instead of me?'

Rather unexpectedly this opportunity had been thrust into my hands, but overwhelmingly I wanted to say 'no'. I had that scrunched-up-tummy feeling that I used to get before swimming galas when I was about ten. I was just enjoying the night as it was. But though I was thinking 'no' and my mind was very sure of that, somehow the words 'Yeah – sure, Rich' tumbled out of my mouth. As the words came out I already wished I could some-how put them back. Was it Rich's persuasive mind-altering powers again that had got us the backstage passes for the comp, or was this a God thing?

Bernard turned to me and leaned towards my ear, asking, 'So, what do you want me to translate?'

'I'm not sure yet,' I replied, as my mind raced through a series of past gospel talks like a receptionist searching through a filing cabinet, looking for a specific document. It was such a privilege to share the gospel, but at the same time the nerves were kick-ing in, and I was unsure as to what would go down well at this type of party scenario.

I opted for the 'extreme Jesus' talk that I had written a couple of years earlier, and after a quick run through with Bernard, we took to the decking. We only had one mic and I feared that it might look as if we were going to sing a duet together. We both leaned towards the mic, holding it clumsily between our pairs of hands. I opened with the question that I shouted with a full breath of air, 'Who wants to live an extreme life?'

The place erupted into cheers and whoops as I gradually

moved on to share the gospel message – a noisy crowd with some faces intently hanging on my every word. The translation flowed meticulously as we took it in turns to lean into the mic to say our next line.

As I came to the conclusion I had no idea how it would end. It didn't seem right to ask people to come and kneel at the bar to accept Jesus. So I left the opportunity hanging and challenged people to come and chat with the team and get prayed for. As I stepped down from the platform, I took a deep breath and patted Bernard on the shoulder.

After a gospel talk, you can often feel very insecure and self-aware. You're never quite sure exactly how it has gone down and everybody kind of looks at you 'funny'.

'You said Jesus can do miracles?' came this one guy. 'Can you pray for my arm?' He looked to be in his late 20s and I couldn't quite place his accent as he raised his arm in my general direction.

Another guy from the UK, kitted out in surf logos, strolled up, saying, 'That took some bottle, bruv. So you believe all that stuff, right?'

'Yep,' I replied as the British guy wandered off nodding his head with a subtle kind of respect. I turned back to the guy with the arm – the bad arm. Immediately, I hit the road running, sharing more of the gospel with a couple of simple analogies. As our short conversation came to an end, I asked if it was cool to lay my hand on the injured arm to pray. His face lit up. He was stoked that someone cared enough to pray for him and with a 'Thanks, mate. That feels much better', he then merged back into the swaying entourage of dancers as the DJ dropped in another tune.

I often find that people love meeting Christians. We have this fear that people will freak out, but so often they are intrigued, especially when we meet them in unexpected places, wearing the same life costumes. After such an intense few minutes, and seeing Bernard chatting to some locals, I searched out a friendly face. I was knackered and needing encouragement. Finding Becky, I wandered over.

Becky was dialoguing with two well-travelled Aussies who were slouched back in the comfort of the decking couch. Her opening comment was about the injuries she had acquired surfing. She pointed to a small red bruise on her knee and told them how much it had hurt.

The Aussies laughed in response and Billy, with a typical Aussie twang, said, 'You call that a surf injury? Check this out!'

He then leaned down and took hold of the bottom of his jeans leg and began to pull it higher and higher, revealing an aesthetic metal pole for a leg with a very realistic-looking foot crafted into his sandal.

The look of embarrassment and total shock on Becky's face was a picture as Billy laughed it off, saying, 'I still have the other one – the great white only got one of them.' I was introduced to the shark attack victim, who still surfed regularly and who had found the fake leg ideal for opening beer bottles on. It turned out that Billy often drank in my local pub, the infamous Raynes Park Tavern, and we promised to hook up later in the year. We never did actually meet up, though I had sent him a Surfers Bible. Incredibly, Becky ended up staying in the same hostel as Billy a year later in Mexico. It is indeed a small world.

I left as Becky began to share her testimony and I decided to climb the towering sand dunes to be alone with God. As I reached the top of the sand dunes to grasp a moment of prayer, I now had a perfect view of the party-goers beneath. In the quieter night air, I knew that I had a deep connection with this place.

It was not merely the surfing or the fact that I had been here before, but it was because my ancestry stems back to France. Somewhere in the distance of time, my ancestors had been Huguenots, French Calvinists who had fled to England under persecution.

I continued to watch Becky with Billy the one-legged surfer. I pondered on what it must take to surf again after such a haunting experience as being attacked by a great white. Every time you get back into the water there must be a sense of trepidation as you remember the fateful day of the attack. But I guess that if you are really passionate about something, then you are willing to do whatever it takes.

The Huguenots had been a passionate people. They had embraced Calvin's reformed theology with its doctrine based on the authority of the Bible rather than church tradition. They had discovered that salvation only comes through the grace of God. From the 1540s, the Calvinist movement had steadily grown, with trained missionaries being sent to plant churches from Geneva.

But Calvinism was seen as heretical by the Catholic Church, which dominated France. With its vast financial resources and its close political ties to royalty, persecution began. Rivalry and battles between the two churches became commonplace, coming to a head at the Massacre of St Bartholomew, in which 12,000 Protestants were slaughtered in an intense season of persecution.

In 1685, laws protecting the Calvinists were withdrawn and the persecution continued. The Huguenots were forbidden to leave the country, but were also banned from worshipping publicly. They were strongly encouraged to convert back to Catholicism. Their church buildings were destroyed. Church readers were beaten and were threatened with financial ruin. Many became martyrs for their faith. Many fled overseas to pursue their faith, leaving family, wealth and homeland.

As I sat on the dune, brimming with these thoughts, I prayed that I, like the Huguenots, might have a greater passion. A passion for my faith that was willing to risk everything in pursuit of God. A passion for those who did not yet know God. I looked back at the party below as people began to head off. I wanted a greater passion for people like these. For people like Simon the Saffa. For people like Billy the one-legged surfer. For people like Max.

* * *

I rejoined the slowly dispersing party, and the conversations continued into the early hours. Tom Curren, our pro-surfer friend, had not turned up, but God had. With a feeling of satisfaction, I pulled down the makeshift screen from the side of the Quiksilver bus and helped clear some of the empty cans that littered the floor. As Bernard said goodnight, Max was already talking about next year's Christian Night. 'Let's talk tomorrow,' I said, as my bed beckoned. Christian Night 2006 was on the cards.

* * *

Robin Gwynn, *Huguenot Heritage*, Sussex Academic Press, 2001.

9

Lost in Translation

It's funny how, when you go on a trip somewhere, it can often be harder to repack your case to return home. I am not quite sure why that is, unless you have bought a whole bunch of new things, which we hadn't. Rich's car was already stuffed to overflowing and we still had more to fit in as we packed up the resources.

The predictable series of goodbyes and hugs followed as the short boarders left to go back to Blighty. Their faces had been transformed from a pale milk-carton white to a golden brown over the week. But I hoped that they had gained much more than a tan; that they had grown deeper in Christ and learned more of God's mission for their lives.

As we were saying goodbye, I could detect that a few of the long boarders, who still had five days left of the three-and-a-half-week long-board mission trip left, were looking rather envious. After almost three weeks of living out of a suitcase, which always starts out as fun, there comes a point when you are wearing the same pair of board shorts for four days in a row. As the smell begins to waft, you begin to miss having somewhere to do your washing and somewhere to sit back and watch TV.

The remaining section of the trip was going to involve much more driving and much less mission. DJ Dave had already left, and cameraman Chris and Sarah the linguist were next to leave. With these members of the team gone, the team dynamic would change, and we still had some 1,300 km to travel back to Faro for our flights home in just five days' time. The only good news was that there would be more space in the vehicles!

We needed an injection of enthusiasm to battle the onslaught of apathy. I sensed that people were feeling that the mission was almost up, so I got to work, setting the team a fresh challenge.

We had been distributing the French Surfer Bibles throughout the week in France, and, with 60 copies left, I summoned the team to walk around Biarritz in prayer, giving them away to surf shop employees. With a barrage of Bibles clutched between arms, they separated into groups and dispersed around the town with the set task in hand. Meanwhile I continued the airport shuttle runs, missing out on the action yet again!

Not particularly relishing yet another drive to the airport, I begrudgingly reminded myself to be a servant leader. Leading mission teams, I have discovered, is as much about giving others opportunities as it is running headlong into them yourself. The key role of an evangelist must be to empower and mobilise others. I had a sneaky feeling that the French Bible distribution would evoke some great stories and I wanted to be a part of them.

The Christian Surfer Bibles looked more like magazines with their glossy front covers, action shots of pro-surfers and world-class waves. The attractively packaged Bible was interspersed with testimonies from pro-riders, shark attack victims and surf industry gurus, each sharing their love for the surf and their love for Jesus. They were perfect for Biarritz where the team had been released to carry out the challenge.

Biarritz is one of those quaint seaside Basque towns that thrive with life in the summer months. The sleepy town has been greatly impacted as the surf industry has blossomed. With one Quicksilver shop opening each week on the Continent, Biarritz has been at the forefront of the surfing revolution and hosts a series of shops adorned with international surf brands and logos.

Opposite the main strip of surf shops stands a mighty church. I had first come to Biarritz during my university days, aged 20. A big messy spring swell and windy conditions had meant the week had been a bit of a disaster. I had come with fellow surfers and our student loans had meant that we had to survive on French baguettes as we camped in the grey and rainy April weather. It was at this church that my friends Katie, Danny and Si had lit a candle and prayed for me, knowing that I was a Christian, though they had no faith themselves. Their spiritual appetite had enticed them into the Gothic building that contrasted greatly with the fashion-conscious shoppers who marched around outside in their designer clothing.

It is always strange when you return to a distant place in very different circumstances. As the old church conjured up a bank of memories, it almost seemed as if it had been a different Andy Frost who had been there all those years ago. Having lost contact with those friends, I decided to enter the great gates of the church and light a candle for them, knowing that they had heard the gospel but had never accepted the truth of Jesus.

Meeting up with the rest of the team, they looked excited as they tucked into paninis with melted cheese dripping from the sides. 'So how did it go?' I asked, as their mouths chewed away, making me feel hungry.

'It was wicked!' exclaimed Hannah, as she began to share a story, her south London accent revving with excitement. 'They were so thankful to have something in their own language. They always get stuff from the States and it's always in English. The fact that it was in French kinda showed that Christians cared. People were well up for them.'

'People thought they looked really good,' shared Oliver, the Austrian businessman, with a beaming smile. He had decided to join us on long board for a couple of days before flying back home. And as Oliver tucked into another bite, an avalanche of stories was shared, with each team member reporting what had gone on.

'The shop assistant at Rip Curl asked for extras and wanted to know where they could buy more from to sell in the shop,' shared Lisa.

'In another shop,' Steve shared, 'it looked as though Christmas had come early. The bored sales assistants started reading the Bibles before we'd even left the shop. It was awesome.'

'Another guy, in the shop round there,' continued Jo, as she pointed towards the winding streets of shops, 'has a Christian Surfer mate who keeps showing him Christian surf movies. So he was pretty shocked when we went in offering him a Surfer Bible. He was well excited to get it though. God is definitely on his case.'

The 'giving away of Bibles' exercise had gone down really well. We were the first team to distribute them and I looked forward to communicating with the Christian Surfer guys who had stepped out in faith to get them printed. They would be mightily encouraged to hear people's responses on the ground level in the surf shops of France.

What a privilege it is to have the Bible in our own language. It is hard to imagine being a follower of Jesus without my own personal copy to annotate with thoughts and questions. But there was a time when the average person had no Bible to equip them in their relationship with God.

For centuries the Bible was only available in Latin, and at a very high cost. Latin was the language of the Roman Empire and it became the dominant language across Europe, in which almost all books were written. John Wycliffe had been the first scholar to attempt a translation of the Latin into English in the mid-fourteenth century. He believed that it was everyone's right to have the Bible in their native tongue. The church suppressed his work and it was not until the Reformation that Bible translation accelerated.

Luther kicked off the Reformation in the mid-sixteenth century and the authenticity of the Bible was central to his theology. He attacked the teachings of the Roman Catholic Church, in particular the non-scriptural beliefs of salvation through sacraments rather than grace. He so passionately believed that people should have the Bible in their own language that he personally set himself to translating it into German. As he worked on a German edition, various scholars got to work on their own translations throughout Europe.

It is William Tyndale we need to thank for the bedrock of the English translation that we have today. His vision for an English Bible was not widely shared after the bishops had banned Wycliffe's edition. He was an adventurer who, in his quest to print the Bible in English, survived shipwreck, loss of manuscripts, betrayal of friends and pursuit by secret agents. He painstakingly translated directly from the Hebrew and Greek, with sponsorship from merchants. Tyndale had to leave for the mainland of Europe to finish the New Testament though. His endeavours cost him his life in October 1536, when he was strangled and burned before finishing the Old Testament. But it was his translation that formed much of the basis for the version printed under King James in 1611.

Too often, I take the Bible for granted. I forget that people laid down their lives for us to have this vital jewel through which we might know God more fully. Even today people risk their lives to smuggle Bibles across borders into closed countries. We were not risking our lives on this Road Trip, but we were a continued part of this story because the Bible was being made available in the language of the day.

The empty plates and glasses marked the end of our meal in the rather strange café we had arranged to meet in. The café was decorated with loads of pagan and Eastern symbols, and as the owner came over to collect our empties, he was intrigued by the remaining three Bibles that lay on the table. Pointing towards them he asked, 'What are these?'

Jo told him what we were doing as we motioned for him to pick one up. As Jo and Lisa shared, he flicked through pages, his eyes absorbing some of the photos that jumped out of the pages. When we told him he could have that copy for free, a broad smile spread across his face and he kept saying thank you again and again. He seemed so thankful, I almost thought he might have torn up the bill. Unfortunately that didn't happen!

It's moments of conversation like that which are often missed as we live busy lives in the hustle bustle of trying to fit everything in. In the normal business of life, we are so rushed that I am sure we miss open opportunities to dialogue with people about their day. God wanted to speak to that café owner, as He wants to speak to everyone, but how often are we aware of what Jesus is doing? I decided that I needed to make my life more open for conversations with strangers.

* * *

With an *au revoir*, we left France and crossed over the almost non-existent border back into Spain, speeding along the toll road towards San Sebastian. When I was about twelve, my parents had packed the car for two weeks and driven to Italy. I remember vividly the tight border control and the stamping of passports as armed guards marched around cars, peeking into the backs of vehicles with suspicious eyes. Europe seems so different today, with its open borders and shifting people groups.

We were soon passing signs for San Sebastian, but decided to keep on going. I had some contacts there, but with difficulties corresponding, as the local church were all on holiday, there was now no real reason for visiting. We decided to head for the sea-line and meander along the green coast that curves around head-lands, offering spectacular views of the open ocean. The beauty of the sea was nicely contrasted with the reality of our financial situation, which Steve was unpacking for me as he sat in the passenger seat giving me the low-down.

Steve had rather unwillingly accepted the joyous role of accountant for the trip. He opened the school notebook that had figures scrawled over dozens of pages, with a list of items that money had been spent on. Wedged into the book was a loose mountain of receipts that wafted every time the book was opened. Steve didn't love the role and I began to think that per-haps this was the real reason for Judas's betrayal. He hated doing the accounts. I just hoped Steve was not plotting my demise!

I always knew that the budget was going to be tight. The money people had paid had quickly been eroded with vehicle hire, petrol costs, tolls, food and accommodation. Steve scratched his head as he made the calculations before nervously giving me the full low-down. 'Well, we're down to our last 250 quid. Can we actually make it on this?' came his remark. With possible payments for a new tyre for the VW and possible fines for accidentally skipping a couple of road tolls, who knew where we would be financially?

I jokingly replied, 'Maybe we could borrow some tights off the girls and do a bank.' Steve didn't laugh – probably because it wasn't overly funny. Staying optimistic, as I generally tend to be, I said, 'It will sort out – it always does.' As I said those words, I knew it was time to start scrimping – maybe a three-day fast?

* * *

Arriving in Santander, we searched for a bargain place to stay and wandered through the streets laden with our rucksacks. We began intense negotiations with the Antipodeans who ran the youth hostel for a local businessman. They had to call the owner to strike deals, but after some classic bartering, we were offered the bargain rate of eight euros per person for a flat that had a dodgy smell and no hot water.

'I'll take it!' I exclaimed. With deals like this, Steve and I could make the books balance – no problem.

We were directed to the other side of town, so we set off, carrying our rucksacks that were nicely engraving strap marks into our shoulders as sweat patches enlarged from beneath our armpits. We arrived at the flat, exhausted, and climbed the four storeys to our apartment.

The apartment had a small balcony that overlooked the street, which was called August 31st. Remarkably the date was August 31st and that night the entire town arrived to parade up the street and light candles in memory of a great fire that had destroyed much of the city. This yearly tradition was something of a spectacle and with local tapas slowly digesting, we moved over to the balcony to get a front row view. All for eight euros!

The staff who were operating the backpackers' apartments turned up to join us as we watched the proceedings unravel beneath. As I looked down the street, hundreds of balconies were shimmering in the light of candles that were lined along the banisters. Lights shining in the darkness. Light piercing the darkness.

'North Spain is a pretty dark place.' I recalled a conversation that I had had with Matt, a missionary from the States. I had met him at the beginning of the year by the beach. We had arranged to meet through Christian Surfers. North Spain can be very different in the winter and I remembered back to the great grey clouds that had engulfed the sky and the snow that had littered the high ground like icing on doughnuts. The town had a very different feel right now as the summer season peaked.

I had gone with Matt to a stereotypically Spanish café, with meat hanging from the roof beams. Sipping on cappuccinos, we had spent time sharing stories and swapping dreams. He was originally from California, another keen surfer who had moved to Spain with a passion to share Jesus. He sat with a radiant face that was slowly transitioning from the wind chill outside to the pleasant warmth of the café. A beanie sat squarely on his head and it almost reached down to his eyebrows, moving in unison every time he spoke. 'Having felt the call to Spain, I came here with my buddy. We thought we would come here for a few months and teach English. My friend then left, but I knew I had to stay.'

Matt was teaching English to support himself and loved

surfing with the local kids while sharing his faith. He spoke about the need for purpose that had drawn many young people into the Basque Separatist movement and how he longed for them to discover Jesus as a cause to live for.

His passion for God shone through as the coffee cup slowly emptied. He had been intensely praying for the Basque region and was greatly encouraged to discover our vision for Road Trip missions. 'Talk about mission field – this place needs Jesus. The church here is so small and the UK is so close. With dirt-cheap air-fares, there's no excuse for not doing more short-term mission over here in Europe. We need help. It's great that you guys are catching on.'

Matt was at home in San Diego during our trip, but as I mentally revisited the conversation that we had had all those months earlier, I knew that we had to spend time here praying.

* * *

'Let's climb it,' I exclaimed, and the group gradually nodded heads and braced themselves for the climb ahead. Right behind where we were staying, there was a large hill with steep sides that led to a church and a massive statue of Jesus reaching for the skies above. It looked like an ideal place to pray and a pace was set as we began the walk, quickly distilling into different groups according to length of stride.

The statue of Jesus above Santander can be seen for miles around. But it's not alone. Throughout Spain, huge statues of Jesus punctuate the skyline. For us, these statues of Jesus were something of an oddity and whenever they were spotted as we drove down motorways, our attention was always drawn. But these gigantic Jesus figurines had probably become very familiar to the locals – a part of their landscape and heritage that perhaps bore little relevance to day-to-day living.

Walking up hills in the heat of the day is exhausting, as the sun seems to sap your energy away. For years now I have been climbing to high places to be alone with God. I know that I can commune with God anywhere, but there seems to be something special about high places. Jesus often climbed hills to be with the Father; the Law was given to Moses on Mount Sinai; and the transfiguration and the crucifixion both took place on high ground.

Perhaps it's the journey element that helps me to focus upon Him – the physical strain acting as a precursor to the prayer. Perhaps it is something similar to the highs and lows of life. I am not sure, but it is at high places that I have often encountered God most powerfully. Not church sanctuaries, but being out in His creation.

Carn Brea is one of my favourite places. It is situated near Redruth, and from the top you can see most of Cornwall. The path meanders upwards from a car park, leaving the twenty-first century behind. Five minutes later, from the towering Celtic cross, you can stand and watch the shadows of the clouds chase their way over the green pastures that are artistically interspersed with tightly packaged urban pockets and old mines.

Four years earlier, I had led a group of young people to this place with a Cornish minister called Steve. Steve is one of those passionate, smiling people, and he has catch phrases such as 'Oh . . . wonderful' and 'Praise the Lord, brother!'. He is a tall, skinny man, around the 50 mark, and he loves to pray.

He enthusiastically recounted the story of the Primitive Methodists in the early nineteenth century. The 'Prims', as they were known, were a movement of Methodists characterised by their depth of spirituality. As Steve told the story of men coming up to Carn Brea to fast and pray, he introduced me to the concept of 'getting faith'.

When the Prims felt that they had a vision from God, they would often ascend somewhere like Carn Brea to 'get faith', the idea being that they would pray and fast, sometimes for days on end, until they felt God had given them the faith to see their vision become reality.

As I shout my intercession from the boulders of granite that adorn the foot of the towering cross at Carn Brea, my faith level slowly rises. In my combats and t-shirt, I must look very different from the generations before me. But I stand with the same dreams and the same Great Commission, my vision always beginning in humility at the foot of the cross.

The beating sun in Santander was very different from the windswept Carn Brea. But as we reached the statue of Jesus, there was a real similarity – the view that stretched out below was an inspiration for prayer. From the Jesus statue in Santander, an urban sprawl of grey loomed into the distance, tightly imprisoned by the blues of the ocean and the green mountains in the distance. From the distance of time, before there was a 'big Jesus' on this hill or a big grey metropolis below, I could imagine people coming here to pray.

As we stood by the feet of Jesus, and as team members continued to reach the breezy climax of the climb, we prayed. With a very different perspective on the world below, I prayed for Matt, for his local church and for all the young people of this place, that they might find the ultimate 'cause' to live for. And then I thanked God for the high places, where I could see a different perspective on the world below: His perspective.

* * *

Tim Dowley, *The History of Christianity*, Lion Publishing, 1990.

Geoffrey Milburn, *Primitive Methodism*, Epworth Press, 2002.

10

Am I Becoming a Monk?

'**H**ere's what I picture when I think of a monastery. I picture a group of men with bowl-shaped haircuts and brown coarse cloaks, drinking dark-brown ale.' I shared my preconceptions as we gradually drove up the valley road which followed a meandering river, dwarfed by the mountains that climbed steeply on either side. Slowly weaving our way along the corridor of concrete, cameras were poised and a repetition of gasps echoed through the vehicles as each turn brought with it ever more stunning views.

As we headed south we had opted for the scenic route and had decided to visit an ancient monastery where monks still live today. We had shared what we expected to find on our arrival. Our common belief was that a Friar-Tuck-type tubby man would be there to greet us with a broad smile and a warm hearty laugh.

It seems that rediscovering monastic living is a cool thing to do at the moment. But though we all knew it was culturally quite cool, we had little idea of what it would look like, especially in a Spanish monastery hiding in the stunning green mountains.

The monastery was not all I'd hoped for. There was no singing group of monks dressed in Jedi-type cloaks to welcome us. It was a pretty ordinary brickwork building, with a very plain general décor, modern windows and a distinct lack of original character. There were a few tourists milling around, buying touristy memorabilia.

But I didn't want to visit as a tourist. I wanted to visit as a pilgrim. I wanted to glean a deeper understanding of what it meant to be a practising monk in the twenty-first century. Wasn't it all about running away from the real world to live a life of escapism? Or were people still called to take up the single life, sacrificing everything to intercede for the world from a mountain top?

We tried to arrange a meeting with the monks with the receptionist at the bookshop. It wasn't just because I wanted my picture taken with an old Spanish dude in a brown flowing garment for the mantelpiece. Although that would have been cool. It was because I wanted to understand this ancient lifestyle choice and to learn from the experience of modern-day monks.

Unfortunately the only way to have a proper chat with a monk was if you were seriously considering a call to monastic life. I didn't feel that calling was for me and the thought of discussing it in Spanish was even less appealing. I could imagine inadvertently signing up and then having to telephone home to tell my parents that I would not be back for a while, explaining, 'Oh, and there'll be no grandkids!'

The monastery was famous in that it claimed to have a segment of the actual cross on which Jesus was crucified. In order to have a look at this ancient relic, you had to sit through a 45-minute liturgical act of worship, complete with sermon, in Spanish. Thinking that we would never again get the opportunity to see such a holy relic, we sat near the back of the vestry with wooden beams and an ornate Communion area covered with lots of purples, reds and gold.

The service, attended by about 30 people, was less than inspiring. In the sweltering heat, high up in the mountains, drowsiness became a big problem. Shuffling continually to keep my eyes from closing, the moment finally came when we could step forward. The queue weaved round the altar as figures bent low to kiss the base of a gold cross containing the wooden fragment encased in glass. This piece of the cross had supposedly been brought to northern Spain by St Peter.

After all that expectancy, it was a bit of an anticlimax. I decided not to kiss the tip of gold. I am not sure why I didn't, but I felt uncomfortable giving this relic that kind of respect. The monk held so tightly to the gold cross and it looked as though he feared someone might snatch it and run at any moment. The crumbly piece of wood that was packed inside the gold cross was very much a non-event to me. It was, after all, just a piece of wood.

Summing up my feelings on monastic life is very difficult. Throughout the centuries, differing theologies have meant that monasteries have had very different emphases. During the fourth to the sixth centuries, monastic leaders left their imprint. Basil was keen that monastic communities should be outwardly focused, and under his influence many began to care for the sick and provide education; Martin of Tours saw monasteries as a springboard for evangelism to reach pagan rural France; Augustine of Hippo called for monastic communities to serve the local church; under Abbot Schnoudi, monks were encouraged to get involved in political warfare, sometimes even murdering pagans and trashing their temples; and then Cassiodorus put an emphasis on the studious copying of manuscripts.

The idea of monastic life began under the Roman Empire. Initially Christians were persecuted for their faith under Roman rule.

As time moved on, Christianity became tolerated and church numbers grew. As their numbers grew, their standards lowered and as standards lowered, some Christians felt that they needed to 'flee the world', as it hindered them from living out their Christian life to the full. They were often individuals who spent time in the deserts of Egypt and Syria. They lived disciplined lives of prayer, meditation and fasting. They were given to a life of celibacy and sometimes went to the extreme of living on the top of pillars in order to grow closer to God.

The Rule of Benedict has become the bedrock of most monastic communities today. Little is known of Benedict, except that he was Italian and studied in Rome before becoming a hermit and establishing several small monasteries. His rule was adopted in Ireland and it was the Irish who went on to re-evangelise Europe in the sixth century. The Rule of Benedict is based upon two disciplines: prayer and work.

It is this idea of discipline that runs through monastic life that I feel the church today needs to rediscover. The concept of learning Scripture by rote, living by a code of conduct and praying at set times may seem overly legalistic, especially to a generation searching for the next feel-good event, but we need to nourish our spirituality. We need to respond to the grace of God, like the monks did, surrendering our lives and giving everything over to Him in the pursuit of holiness.

As we left the monastery, homeward bound, the challenge to live in the everyday monotony as a bond-slave to Christ convicted my very essence. Maybe abandonment would be easier hidden away on the mountainside, but I have been called to live as Christ in the world.

* * *

The repetition of streetlights shooting overhead with the hum-drum sound of tyres cruising over the weathered concrete was a recipe for sleepiness. My eyes were focused intently on the cat's eyes that led the way ahead. My hunched shoulders and aching back cried out for rest. I felt so tired that I pinched myself to stay awake. After a day of almost continuous driving, we had been trying to find somewhere to stay for the last two hours, but with no joy. I was now desperate to pull over and sleep. Anywhere would do. My eyelids were so heavy that it was like fighting back an incoming tide. Impossible. The countless Cokes and coffees had lost their edge and a polluted caffeine-induced sickly feeling was rising in my stomach. Even the open widow with its blasts of cool air was failing to help me focus.

Spotting a sign for a National Park, I knew that this was my opportunity. We swung off at the exit and headed past the National Park sign and into the darkness. No cat's eyes. No overhead streetlights. Just the full beam, which lit up the forested path as it got narrower by the mile. The winding roads and the change in momentum caused my fellow pilgrims to stir. Only Jo had managed to stay awake with me and she leaned forward in her seat, with her eyes meticulously reviewing each turn, to look for somewhere to pull in.

'There has got to be an opening here to sleep in,' I exclaimed. 'I am knackered.' Three or four miles down the track, I was beginning to think that I had made a big error coming into the National Park, as the road was bordered by heavy vegetation but nowhere to set up camp. As I began to work through the logistics of a three-point turn off the narrow road in a VW, which would probably have been more like a 20-point turn, we suddenly chanced upon a small opening.

Before Jo had time to tell me, I was already parked and taking off my seatbelt. With the door swung open, I threw myself out of the van and raised my arms to the air to fully stretch my body. Driving in the hunched-over position for so long, I almost felt six inches shorter. As I stretched, I could feel the various bones in my spine click back into place. The van lights lit the foreground of rocks that stretched about eight metres before dropping into deep vegetation.

'Sorry, guys, but I am too tired to keep driving. We are going to have to stay here tonight.'

Slightly unimpressed faces exited from the vehicles as the team gathered in the light of the van and viewed the rocky surface before them. No comfy hotel tonight then.

'Shot gun the van,' shouted Jon, who had lost his sleeping bag and was now sleeping in a surfboard bag!

As Steve brushed his teeth in the light of the VW with bottled water, I scrambled past and got my sleeping bag. My teeth could wait. As my feet kicked away the bigger rubble that laced the ground, I lay my sleeping bag down in position. A bit of bug spray for my neck and I was set for some well-earned dreams.

As I crouched on the sleeping bag and turned my head upwards, I suddenly felt as if I was in a different world. The perfectly clear sky was brimming with thousands of stars. In that instant, the tiredness began to ebb. 'Look up, guys. Look at the stars. It's absolutely insane.' I sounded like an excited seven-year-old when the Christmas tree lights are put on for the first time. We would have missed this vast display of shining stars if we had not stopped. As I gazed up into the abyss, fellow pilgrims came and lay near me, slipping into their sleeping bags and fixing their eyes on the sky above.

The tiredness was now completely gone. Normally I hate it when that happens, but tonight I had an amazing ceiling to wonder at. With faces gawping upwards, the uncomfortable ground had almost gone unnoticed.

'Apparently, in medieval times, they used to believe that the night sky was one thick black canvas with holes. They believed that the glory of God was behind it and that it was this light that shined through the holes, creating what we call stars.' I shared my random thought as a shooting star flashed across the sky and the team yelped in excitement. I played it cool, having watched many meteorite showers before.

Looking up and watching stars is a really soothing activity. For me, watching the night sky puts life into perspective, showing me just how insignificant I really am and just how vast God is. That night, my little insecurities and worries about finance and team dynamics drained from my head and a sense of awe encapsulated me.

The air was silent, as we were several miles from the nearest road, and there was no artificial light for some distance. A show of shooting stars commenced, and bursts of 'Did you see that one?' interrupted prayers of adoration and thanksgiving that seemed so much more tangible out under the stars. We were lost in wonder at God's creation. Then a meteorite ripped through the atmosphere and burst into flames. I had never seen anything like that before and I erupted into, 'That one was blooming crazy – absolutely mental,' instantly losing my more laid-back approach. The team laughed at my childish excitement. Then the laughter turned to whispers. The whispers turned to silence. And the silence turned to sleep.

* * *

'Andy, what was that? Andy?'

I awoke to the worried voice calling my name.

'What?' I replied, sitting bolt upright.

'I heard a noise. What was it?' replied Hannah, her voice full of worry.

'I don't know. Go back to sleep,' I replied as I lay back down, nestling into the groove of the rough terrain.

A screeching noise filled the quiet night air and Hannah again called out, 'Andy, what *is* that?' In the midst of a strange place with strange sounds, it is easy for the imagination to begin to run wild. The noise was definitely unnerving. I thought about doing my manly courageous duty – climbing out of my sleeping bag, wandering round the area with a torch and then reassuring Hannah that everything was going to be OK – but, well, to be honest, I was too tired. 'It's probably a monster coming to get you,' I replied in a rather sarcastic voice. 'Go back to sleep.'

Hannah's alarm began to wake others as she threatened, 'Andy, if you don't tell me what that is, I'll get back in the van.' The panic that was growing in her voice meant that I had to take this more seriously. The thought of waking up with rabid foxes or a huge bear munching its way through a team member did cross my mind, but I was so tired that all I could do was laugh at the situation. I was warm, and felt irrationally secure in my all-season sleeping bag.

'Don't worry, Hannah,' I said. 'There are six of us sleeping out, so even if we are attacked, the odds are pretty much in your favour.'

As other team members listened in on our conversation, laughter rippled from the sleeping bags. Then the noise came again – louder and seemingly closer. The unfamiliar screeching sound could have been anything, for all I knew. My GCSE Biology all those years ago hadn't covered 'dangerous animal noises in Spanish forests'. I could define 'evapo-transpiration', but that wasn't overly relevant right now.

The sound screeched through the forests again.

'Andy? Andy!' came Hannah again, awaiting orders for the next military manoeuvre.

'What do you want me to do?' I replied. 'I am not sure what that noise is, but I recommend you go back to the van if you are too worried to sleep outside. I am going to stay out here. It's probably animals mating. But it's your call.'

Hannah quickly stood up, gathering her pillow and sleeping bag, and got back into the van. The other team members began to think about piling into the already overcrowded van too, but I reassured them, 'I am staying out – we'll be fine.'

It's funny how fear of the unknown can shape how we live our lives. As I snuggled back into my groove, I thought back to the original monks who had gone to live alone in the desert. Records show that these monks sometimes had experiences of combating demons. Whether they were real or whether they were induced by a lack of water and extreme heat, I am not sure. But there is something about going to face our fears that we have lost in a sanitised culture in which we need to write a risk assessment before leaving the house. Just as Jesus went into the wilderness to face His temptation, maybe each of us needs to find our personal wilderness.

I closed my eyes, knowing that there were now only five of us sleeping beneath the stars. If we were attacked, one in five was still pretty good odds, I thought selfishly.

* * *

Back in Faro and the journey had taken its toll. We arrived to the clean white sheets of a more up-market hotel than when we had first arrived. It is amazing how, when you arrive at a hotel, it is always so clean, especially when you have been travelling and sleeping rough. Hot showers cleansed us of the dirt from the ground the night before and I watched as brown water disappeared through my toes and down the plug hole.

Being back in Faro, it felt as if we had been gone for months rather than three weeks. We gathered on the veranda of one of the hotel rooms, feeling much cleaner and fresher. I had gathered everyone together to share their thoughts and views of the trip. Reflection is an essential part of any pilgrimage or mission trip and it is something that we often overlook. It is vital to bring closure to a trip as feelings and insights are shared. This was an important part of ending our journey.

A loose circle of white plastic chairs was arranged and with an obvious shortage of seats, Jo and Jon opted to sit on the wall and Steve crouched on the floor. With eyes fastened on me, I opened up, 'Well, guys, here is where the adventure began and here is where it comes to a conclusion. What a trip – eh?'

Nods, smirks and utters of 'yeah' echoed their agreement, so I continued, 'I think it would be really cool just to share some of our highs and lows of the trip. How have you been challenged to change? What has God been saying? That kind of stuff. . .'

The girls laughed because it turned out that they had already had this conversation. Jon and I had needed to sleep off the drive that had taken us right across Spain and into Portugal, but the girls had managed to sleep on the journey and had gone off for coffee in the afternoon to chat through the trip. Slightly aggrieved that they had not waited for Jon, Steve and me to be a part of that conversation, I asked them what they had come up with.

Jo started the ball rolling: 'For me, I've got a bigger perspective on mission. I think sometimes we have such a constricted definition, but as a community travelling, I hope that people have seen Christ in us throughout.'

'It's how church should be,' interrupted Hannah, gaining immediate eye contact with me. 'Being community and witnessing 24-7, even when we're just hanging out getting food.'

Becky nodded in agreement as she played with her brown curly hair. 'I love this team. It's been so awesome getting to know you all and sharing this adventure with you. I feel like we have bonded so well and that God has been leading us, and that's just cool.'

The conversation moved on to highlights and it was intriguing to hear different people's top moments. For Lisa, it had undoubtedly been meeting the Italians for the second time. It had revealed to her something more of God's grace and His overview. For Jo, it had been Cape St Vincent, where she had done business with God and captured something of a greater vision for Europe. For Jon, it had been hanging out with the Uhlers and sharing in their local mission. A colourful spectrum of memories was slowly distilling into our long-term memory banks.

'I think for myself,' I shared, 'I can't separate one specific highlight. For me the journey as a whole, sharing in a dream with you guys, has been great. I have enjoyed reconnecting in a new way with the past, with the lives of people who died years ago. Also reconnecting with different Christian traditions that have challenged me to rethink aspects of my theology. You know, I thought that we were pioneering missionaries, but in fact history does repeat itself. And this gives me faith, because God can use us as ordinary people to shape history now.'

My 'comment' was becoming more like a speech at winning an Oscar as I went on: 'Thank you for joining me; thank you for taking the risk to come on this adventure; thank you for throwing yourselves into the plans of God.' Then gaining eye contact with Steve, I added jokingly, 'And best of all, we have done it in budget. Just!'

I really was thankful to the team – these were not the shallow words that we can often use in Christian gatherings. I had felt the call to the mainland of Europe, and the Road Trip brainchild was a risky change in missional tack from previous years. However, God had been faithful and people had stepped up to the challenge. Remembering His faithfulness makes it much easier to dream for God next time round. I know that the more I dream for God, the more I step out into the unknown. But I also know that He is with me.

'It's also revolutionised the way I see travelling,' continued Steve. 'I love to travel – but this has been travelling with purpose. It's not been all about us. Each day there has been an opportunity to serve and to communicate Jesus, even in the simplest of stuff.'

'Yeah,' continued Lisa, as she momentarily looked quite serious, 'I want to start carrying tracts every day, because I think there are so many opportunities we miss because we forget that we are on mission.'

Each mission that I have been on has led to a fresh motivation to live a more mission-minded life. People seem to be challenged to do this, not by going to a nice seminar and talking about it, but by actually living it. Throwing a hand grenade into the pleasantries, I asked, 'But we have not seen anyone definitely make a commitment to Christ – is that not an issue?'

Stunned silence hit the group for a moment as stark reality caused eyes to focus on the floor in thoughtfulness. Ellie broke the silence with her wise rhetorical question, 'But surely that is God's job?' You could tell she was studying at Durham!

'Absolutely,' Jo continued, 'but I am not fully satisfied. I still want to see more, and what else do we need to do to see more of God at work?'

'That sounds like a call to prayer, Jo,' I said with a very cheesy grin.

We had not been able to meet the monks, but perhaps we didn't need to. Perhaps Road Trip had been monastic without us even realising it. A natural rhythm of prayer and a rhythm of witness had flowed throughout. We were just friends sharing a journey with God, sharing our things and sharing life with each other.

As everyone stepped forward from their chairs, arms interlinked over shoulders and the group morphed into a tight circle of friends. We began to pray. This is where every adventure and every mission should begin and end: in prayer with friends. There were prayers of thanks for all that God had done. There were prayers of adoration for all that we had seen. And then there were prayers of desperation, that we might do 'greater things than these', that they may be done in Europe, and that they may be done in our generation.

As I slouched back in my chair, the meeting drew to a natural close and pockets of conversation opened up. The trip was officially over and I looked forward to some time alone to process my thoughts. The three weeks of intense activity had left my mind shell-shocked. Over the coming months, seasoned with prayer, I could dream the next phase of the adventure. For the adventure was not over. It was merely beginning.

* * *

Flights home and pilgrims return. Empty wallets, dirty laundry, saturated with story. No longer spectators but wide-eyed adventurers. Convicted . . . challenged . . . now catalysts for change. Big-picture idealists with a vision for the nations and a passion for the lonely.

Continue to walk in the footsteps of ancient heroes. Times change. Wrinkles appear. Experiences become memories. Memories become photos in online albums. But the adventure never ends. History books of the future wait to be written. The world is your oyster. The car door is open. The command is to 'Go'. . .

* * *

Dietrich Bonhoeffer, *The Cost of Discipleship*, SCM Press, 2001.

Tim Dowley, *The History of Christianity*, Lion Publishing, 1990.

Epilogue

A year on and I sit sieving these memories into a laptop, surrounded by empty Coke cans. I am preparing to go back to the Crème Café in France in a week's time and I am not sure where this story will end up. I am still living in the unknown of what God will do next. I remain ever expectant and ever hungry that we would see those bold prayers that we prayed at St Vincent answered.

God has drawn me back to the Continent a couple of times since the Road Trip and there is one instance that stands out. I was at a gathering of twenty-somethings who are engaged in mission and church planting. The weekend was set in the historic city of Berlin and we spent time sharing stories, listening to God and praying together.

The one instance that stands out was taking Communion with a young German lady. As we took Communion together, I prayed for Germany and she prayed for the UK. We lifted up our countries to God with quiet whispers as people dispersed around the bare hall to pray in pairs.

As we prayed, tears began to roll down her face and cascade to the wooden floor below, creating miniature puddles. I am never good with 'emotional' women and almost scurried off with a 'need to go to the loo' get-out clause.

But as she cried she looked into my eyes and said, 'We need you.' The sleeve of her black top brushed the tears away and smudged mascara darkened her cheeks.

I was slightly taken aback by her comment, but as we talked this weeping German lady explained that she believed the UK needs to assist the church in Europe in re-evangelising the Continent. The UK needed to stop being so inwardly focused and to see the wider perspective.

Her humble request for support has been with me ever since. Those simple words, 'We need you.'

And so I continue to dream for Europe.

And I continue to pray for Europe.

And I long for the day when Britain rediscovers its missionary-sending history.

God seems to have captured my heart and I can't shake it off. These dreams long for a reality. The stage is set and awaits brave adventurers who will step up to the challenge.

The patchwork of stories from this trip, and the stories that fill our history books, remind me of His faithfulness. God has dreams and He longs for us to be a part of them. Maybe we need to stop thinking within our own possibilities. Maybe we need to see the bigger picture. After all, God is not British. He doesn't speak the Queen's English and I doubt He wears a bowler hat. Our God is a God of the nations and He longs for the nations to enter into a relationship with Him. But who will go?

This adventure begins on our doorstep and could take us anywhere. It simply begins with 'Here I am Lord, send me.' You may end up speaking to clubbers, playing with orphans, on the beach with pro-surfers, or hanging out with heroine addicts in the slums. Or you may end up dialoguing over a business lunch in Frankfurt with suited and booted entrepreneurs, or lecturing to students in Estonia, or meeting governmental agencies in Brussels.

Anything can happen when your heart lives for adventure . . . when your heart is open to the plans of God.

Survivor Music

Emerging Culture: (£6.99)

This recording aims to take the Emerging Culture worship experience and make it relevant to worshipping God throughout the year. An encouragement not just for a week-long event but an on-going season of worship. Newcastle rock worship team Yfriday & Emerging Culture worship teams The Cedars & Echolab all feature on this snapshot of worship from Emerging Culture '06. A combination of fresh sounds and songs from Emerging Culture feature on this 8 track emerging event album.

Universal: Yfriday, (£12.99)

Yfriday have developed into one of the most prominent bands in the UK. Faithfully they have served churches and events with their own brand of worship. They have inspired many young Christians in their faith. Universal brings themes of the grace and magnificence of God right through to God's hunger for justice on earth. The band still deliver God inspired themes through a huge wall of sound!

Underdogz: The 29th Chapter, (£12.99)

The 29th Chapter deliver a fresh, unique Hip-Hop sound with outstanding performances. They combine their musical influences and styles to bring together a unique blend of sounds and flavours. The 29th Chapter is a movement of four individuals whose aim is to perform a distinctive and engaging show that will reach young people with the life changing message of Jesus.

www.survivor.co.uk

Survivor books...receive as you read

Survivor Books came out of a desire to pass on revelation, knowledge, experience and lessons learnt by lead worshippers and teachers who minister to our generation.

We pray that you will be challenged, encouraged and inspired and receive as you read.

Worship, Evangelism, Justice:
Mike Pilavachi & Liza Hoeksma (£6.99)

We know that worship is much more than singing songs to God. Don't we? This book looks at what happens when we let Worship infuse all areas of our lives, what Evangelism looks like in today's culture, and what God's passion for Justice means in a broken and hurting world. God holds all three close to his heart: if we bring them back together, could we regain the lost voice of the church?

The Smile of God: Andy Hawthorne (£6.99)

You can't win God's favour - it's been won for you. But you can live in such a way that you know his smile on your life.

If you're tired of conforming to the pattern of the me-centred world, if you're open to the disciplines and the passions of a real man or woman of God, if you're ready to trust God in times of discouragment or outright opposition, then let this book kick start, or fire you up again. God's smile awaits you.

Diary of a Dangerous Vision:
Andy Hawthorne (£6.99)

The story of Andy Hawthorne's dramatic conversion and the adventure of an ever-growing group of Christians set to take Christ into the most and tough urban areas. Their vision spawned a number of different related initiatives: the beginning and the growth of The World Wide Message Tribe, Cameron Dante's conversion, and the EDEN project in Manchester. Reading this book will leave you challenged and inspired.

Eden: Called to the Streets: Matt Wilson (6.99)

Something is happening in our cities. A quiet miracle. Followers of Jesus are moving out of their comfort zones. Leaving old securities behind, they plant their homes and their souls in urban community. Young and old, single and married... they choose to live out their lives in the face of some of the highest rates of crime, social deprivation, drug and alcohol abuse and unemployment. Matt Wilson tracks this amazing story of Eden in Manchester, from early beginnings in the 1990s to the brink of a whole new generation of disciples on the streets.

www.survivor.co.uk

Survivor books...receive as you read

God on the Beach: Michael Volland (£6.99)
Newquay: the UK's infamous summer party capital. The town heaving with young clubbers and surfers, each one desperate to live life to the full, eager for experience, ready to ride the waves and hit the heights. Into this chaotic carnival dropped Michael Volland, dj, surfer, and team member in a beach mission 21st century style. There was just one problem, Michael was not at all sure that God would turn up.

The Lord of the Ring: Phil Anderson (£6.99)
In 1999, the remarkable and accidental 24-7 prayer movement began. The inspiration was a visit by founder Pete Greig to Herrnhut in Germany, when in the eighteenth century Count Zinzendorf initiated the Moravian prayer watch which ran without ceasing for a hundred years. This is Zinzendorf's story, told through the eyes of a pair of twenty-first century pilgrims seeking to rediscover it afresh. Part biography and part road-trip, it brings the history into vibrant life, while raising deeply prophetic challenges about life and faith today.

Red Moon Rising: Pete Greig (£7.99)
24-7 is at the centre of a prayer revival across the globe and this book gives a fantastic insight into what God is doing with ordinary prayer warriors. Read inspiring stories of people finding a new depth of heartfelt prayer and radical compassion.

City Changing Prayer: Debra & Frank Green (£6.99)
Imagine a regular city-wide gathering of Christians united and focused in prayer. Imagine a church that serves local institutions, and asks nothing in return. Imagine the crime rate falling; teenagers praying; people beginning to believe that there's something in this thing called prayer. Frank and Debra Green have seen all this and more over the past ten years. They have learnt lessons about how to foster mutual trust and spiritual fruitfulness, overcoming the obstacles both inside and outside the church family.

www.survivor.co.uk